Praise for
A Return to I

"It has always been an obsession of Judith's to find the best ingredients for the best dishes. With *A Return to Ireland*, Irish cookery has come of age. Her recipes are steeped in our history and the future of Ireland. From nature to plate, with amazing stories of passion and love from the homeland."

— **Chef Noel McMeel,** executive chef of the 5-Star
Lough Erne Hotel and author of *Irish Pantry*

"Judith's continual passion for Ireland, Irish food and the Irish culture continues to be an inspiration to me and to everyone who meets her here in Georgia. Her zest for life, her stories and her Irish creations in the kitchen are superb and really fun. We have cooked together and shared many memorable meals together and as such we are all drawn to Ireland. It gives me great joy to endorse her long-anticipated second book. May this book inspire and continue to call people to return to Ireland."

— **Chef Ford Fry,** restauranteur and author of *Tex-Mex Cookbook*

"Ireland is an island now renowned for its food, but there was a time when hunger stalked our land, leading many Irish emigrants to flee to America to build new lives for themselves there. They and their descendants created unique bonds between our two countries based on a shared culture and an interlocking history. Judith's beautiful book deftly explores the Irish immigrant story—her own, that of her grandparents, and of the wider Irish-American community—through the medium of recipes passed down through the generations. These now make their way back across the Atlantic in *A Return to Ireland*."

— **Daniel Mulhall,** Ambassador of Ireland to the United States of America

"'We are what we eat,' as the old adage goes. Our culinary traditions and recipes not only link us across time and space to those who came before us, but through us they are kept alive for those who might follow. McLoughlin's new book is a truly intergenerational exploration of one Irish family's emigrant journey from the rugged hills of Ireland to the shores of New England and the tastes of home they've savored ever since. Do yourself a favor and *Return to Ireland* without ever leaving your kitchen."

— **Nathan Mannion,** Head of Exhibitions and
Programmes at EPIC, the Irish Emigration Museum

"The legacy of St. Patrick continues to inspire generations of Irish-Americans to discover the culture of Ireland, and with it the cuisine of Ireland that has been changing so much over the years. Judith's inspirational food and storytelling is very much part of this phenomenon that is calling the Irish diaspora home to Ireland to follow in the footsteps of their ancestors."

— **Dr. Tim Campbell,** director of the St. Patrick's Center

A Return to Ireland

A culinary journey from America to Ireland

A Return to
Ireland

A culinary journey from America to Ireland

Judith McLoughlin

Improve your life. Change your world.

Hatherleigh Press is committed to preserving and protecting the natural resources of the earth. Environmentally responsible and sustainable practices are embraced within the company's mission statement.

Visit us at www.hatherleighpress.com and register online for free offers, discounts, special events, and more.

A RETURN TO IRELAND

Library of Congress Cataloging-in-Publication Data
is available upon request.
ISBN: 978-1-57826-935-8

COVER AND INTERIOR DESIGN BY
CORINNE KUTZ AND CAROLYN KASPER
PHOTOGRAPHY BY GARY MCLOUGHLIN

Printed in the United States
10 9 8 7 6 5 4 3 2 1

Contents

Introduction

A Return to Ireland

Several years ago, I began a new journey with my first book, entitled *The Shamrock and Peach*. That book was the culmination of my dream to tell the Scots-Irish immigrant story through the language of really good food and little did I know how successful this book would be. I had no idea as a new author, how this book would work, but after many copies, two editions and print runs, I am amazed where it has taken me, and all the people I have met along the way.

Fortunately, I have been able to cook and travel all over the United States, from my home base in Atlanta, to the Music City of Nashville. From the snowy Colorado mountains to the red rock canyons of Arizona. From the sunbelt of Florida to the bright lights of New York City where I had the incredible experience and privilege to represent Irish cooking with my dear friends Chef Noel McMeel and author Margaret Johnson at the James Beard House.

It is truly a joy to get to share my love of good food and Irish hospitality with others. Ireland is known the world over for its wonderful hospitality, so it is only natural for me to share that story through my food and my love for people.

One of the completely unexpected side effects of my cooking travels was meeting so many people who asked to travel to Ireland and Scotland with me to see those Celtic lands through my eyes. People read the story of the Scots-Irish, tasted my food and were curious to visit. In time, I followed through and began leading groups of folks from all over this vast United States to Ireland and Scotland, and this has become a great joy in my life. Sharing the beauty and culture of the Celtic lands with my friends helped form the genesis of this book you are now reading. The overflow of excitement and joy felt by Irish Americans as they return to Ireland to visit the land of their ancestors is incredibly precious and moving. The look of wonderment on their faces when they step onto the Giants Causeway, or when they visit Saint Patrick's grave, or when they taste our wonderful seafood whilst gazing out at the Atlantic

from our rugged Irish coastline is truly amazing, and led me to a simple conclusion—Atlantic migration, for so long a painful and tearful experience as Irish people left home, never to return, has now become a joyful experience for their ancestors as they return home.

Irish migration is now in greater numbers going from west to east as Americans desire to experience and own a small piece of the land revered by their forebears. It is a return to Ireland.

During this period of revelation, my husband and I also researched our own family trees and in so doing I came across a startling discovery. Exactly one hundred years before Gary and I left Northern Ireland for America, my great grandparents also made that same journey. We left Ireland for Boston in 1996, and they left Ireland for Boston in 1896—however, they bucked an almost universal trend in that even though they immigrated as poor Irish, they returned to Ireland from America. In their day, virtually no-one did this, but they did. Their story is unusual and startling, and in some way a metaphor for what is happening today, so I decided to use their amazing story as a hook to hang my story on.

In our overly fast world here in America, dominated by technology and loss of identity, it is good to slow down a little and consider our roots. To dive into the culture of Ireland expressed through some amazing food that you in turn can share with those you love. That is the very essence of this book—that you will find inspiration in these pages to share love around the table as we Irish have been doing for centuries.

So, pull up a chair, and let's cook and return to Ireland together!

—Slainte, Judith

The Water is Wide

Recipes based on dishes brought to the New World by Irish settlers

The first Scots Irish settlers arrived in America on six ships. Led by Reverend James McGregor, son of Captain McGregor of Magilligan, County Londonderry in the northwest of Ireland, the ships landed on the north shore of Massachusetts in August 1718.

They'd left the shores of Ireland for many reasons—religious freedom, escape from prejudice, burdensome taxes, and lack of opportunity. These pioneering settlers would go on to establish Londonderry, New Hampshire, the first of many such-named towns in the New World.

Millions of Irish immigrants would follow in their footsteps over the centuries to come, building a new culture in America—one rich with music, stories, faith, family, and perhaps most importantly, food.

One of those immigrant stories belongs to my great grand-parents, John and Etta.

Leaving Ireland

Andrew McGarvey was born in the west of Ireland in 1847; a year the Irish called Black '47, at the height of the Great Famine, also referred to as the Great Hunger.

This was a time in Irish history when poverty and lack of opportunity strangled remote communities, leaving many families struggling to survive. Despite its geographical proximity to what was then the wealthiest, most powerful nation on earth, much of Ireland itself was a poor, rural backwater. In those more remote, agrarian communities, one would find much profound natural beauty, but little in the way of opportunities to make a decent living.

The west of Ireland in particular, suffered because the land was poor to start with. The potato blight meant that many had to eat grass. There is a road in County Mayo called The Hungry Road where the starving people literally crawled along to beg for food or to get on a ship. Those who were able to get to soup kitchens had to build stone walls, often leading nowhere, to

A RETURN TO IRELAND

qualify for the food. The countryside is covered in these walls. Soup spoons are still found buried because of the shame of having to accept alms.

Like many of his fellow countrymen and women, Andrew struggled throughout his life to shake off the legacy of those bleak years. In 1866, he married Mary Jane, his hometown sweetheart. And by the 1870s, he had managed to purchase and work two flax spinning wheels that provided fibers for the weaving industry in Donegal—some of which are still thriving in Donegal Town today.

Andrew and Mary Jane would also go on to have three strong children, including my great-grandmother, Etta.

Etta was a slight, fine-featured young lady who was not afraid of hard work, but struggled with the sheer remoteness of Donegal. As a grown woman without land to inherit, Etta knew that if she wanted more for her life, then she would either need to find a husband of means or find new opportunity in a different land. She chose the latter, and on her 21st birthday, made the fateful decision to leave her close-knit family, and her beloved Ireland, and take a chance on America.

The wide Atlantic beckoned Etta, and in 1896, she boarded a ship in Derry bound for the grand city of Boston.

What must she have felt following through on such a decision? Taking such a brave leap in the dark without a parachute. No welfare, no second chances. Just a few pounds in her pocket, a small suitcase with a change of clothes, and her wits about her.

One year later, a young farmer's son working the land in the beautiful Mourne Mountains area of County Down decided that he, too, needed something more than what his rural Irish life was offering.

John McNeill was the youngest child in a large family of eleven, born in 1874 in the town of Aughlisnafin (og-LISH-na-fin). His father, also named John McNeill, was a sturdy old man with a strong back and a strong faith but a very small farm, a mere 30 acres. Ten other children in the brood forced young John to think about how he could make it in this world. His father worked hard, but in Ireland at the time, a lack of land meant a lack of opportunity.

At 23 years old, young John decided that his best bet was taking a chance on a new life in America. He was good

with his hands, knew how to work the land, knew how to survive. So, he left everything and boarded a ship in Belfast bound for Liverpool. From there, it was a steamer bound for Boston.

One hundred years later, I would walk the path of John and Etta, feeling the same fear and excitement that comes with leaving your home place for new life in a new land.

I left Ireland for Boston in 1996, exactly one century after my great grandparents, bringing my memories with me, and bringing some of my homeland's recipes too.

Favorite foods of Irish people that reflect the wealth of Irish produce and culture, including seafood essentials, farm fresh produce and, of course, dishes created from our beloved potatoes. Enjoy these wonderful recipes, steeped in Irish culture, age-old Irish recipes that immigrants would have loved and carried with them across the wide Atlantic.

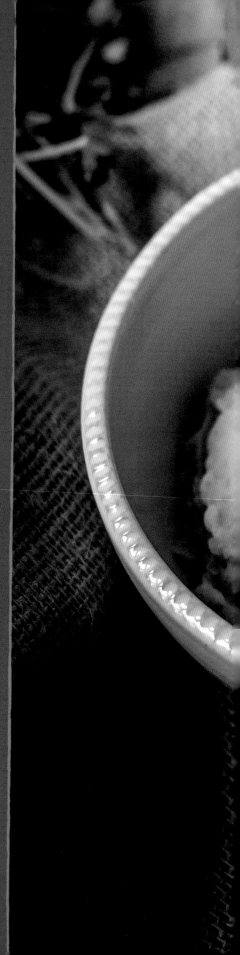

CHAPTER ONE
Irish Immigrant Foods

Emerald Ulster Potato Champ
(page 28)

Wild Atlantic Smoked Salmon Topped Savory Pancakes

Serves 4

Scotch pancakes, also known as "drop scones," are like American pancakes but much firmer with a thicker constancy. They are a perfect base for savory or sweet toppings. Early Irish immigrants would have cooked dropped scones on a griddle, over an open fire, and brought this technique to the new world during the 18th century migrations. Scones, originated in Scotland and the 'Scotch pancake' is now just one of its many forms.

My grandmother used to serve them for afternoon tea with butter, freshly squeezed lemon juice and a sprinkling of sugar or with homemade strawberry preserves. Savory or sweet they are always a treat, and no doubt would have formed an important staple in the farmhouses of those brave immigrants as they built a life for themselves in this brave new world.

For this recipe, I have added wild Atlantic smoked salmon as the topping. It is a delicious addition to complement the pancake, with a touch of crème fraiche and lemon. Smoked salmon is a food loved by Irish people everywhere and always. Enjoy!

PANCAKE INGREDIENTS

6 ounces (1⅓ cup) of self-rising flour
1 teaspoon of baking powder
½ teaspoon sugar
1 egg (beaten)
7 fluid ounces of milk
Pinch of salt
Butter and a little vegetable oil for frying

TOPPING INGREDIENTS

Smoked salmon
Ground black pepper
Olives (chopped)
Sprigs of dill
Crème fraiche
Squeeze of lemon juice

HOW TO MAKE

1. Sift the flour with the baking soda, salt and sugar in a bowl and make a well in the center.

2. Whisk the egg and milk together and pour into the center of the dry ingredients, stirring until combined.

3. In a heavy based pan or griddle, add a just a little butter and vegetable oil. Using a small ladle drop a small amount on to the hot pan. When one side is golden flip over and cook the other side. Remove and set aside.

4. To assemble, pile a little smoked salmon on top of each pancake with a squeeze of lemon juice over the salmon and freshly ground black pepper. Top with a little crème fraiche, chopped olives, and a sprig of dill. Best served right away!

Paddy's Potato & Leek Soup with a Chive Purée & Crunchy Croutons

Serves 4–6

Creamy, silky potato soup may be one of the most traditional Irish dishes, thanks to those beloved root vegetables so famous the world over as the definitive food of the Emerald Isle. Leeks are also common, and their oniony bites are a welcome foil to the velvety potato base.

Irish pubs everywhere have some version of potato soup on their menu, and it is easy to see why. For such a rich, nourishing dish, the ingredients are relatively cheap, and few things warm the belly and the spirit quite as well on a cold winter night.

The green fields and mountains of home seem a little closer with my take on this classic Irish recipe. Fragrant leeks are simmered slowly with potatoes and chicken stock, and then emulsified with cream. It is the ultimate taste of Ireland, and pairs perfectly with a hearty pint of stout and a roaring fire in the hearth. As they say in Ireland, "good stick to your ribs grub!"

SOUP INGREDIENTS

4 ounces (½ cup) salted butter
1 medium onion (diced)
2 large leeks, sliced (use mainly the white part)
5 medium potatoes (4 cups, peeled and diced)
2½ pints chicken stock
1 teaspoon kosher salt
⅛ teaspoon freshly ground pepper
½ cup heavy cream

SPRING ONION PURÉE INGREDIENTS

4 spring onions (chopped)
2 tablespoons canola oil
2 tablespoons salted butter
Fine sea salt

FOR THE GARLIC & HERB CROUTONS

2 slices of baguettes (cut into cubes)
4 tablespoons salted butter
1 tablespoon of parsley (finely chopped)

HOW TO MAKE

1. Start by prepping the leeks. Cut off the root and end and the tough darker green ends and discard them. The white and the lightest green parts are best for the soup. Cut through the leeks from top to bottom and then slice crosswise. To remove any dirt trapped in the leeks, place them in a bowl filled with cold water so the unwanted dirt will sink to the bottom. Using a slotted spoon dry the leeks on paper towels.

2. In a heavy based saucepan melt the butter over low heat. Add the leeks and onions allowing them to "sweat" until they are fragrant.

3. Add the stock and potatoes and season with salt and pepper.

4. Stir to combine on medium heat and bring to a boil. Cover and then turn the temperature down allowing the soup to gently simmer for about 20–25 minutes or until the potatoes are soft.

5. Allow the soup to cool slightly before using an emulsion blender to smooth.

6. To make the spring onion purée, blanch the spring onions in salted boiling water for just less than 1 minute. Strain and place in ice water. Transfer to a blender to purée with a little oil. Pass the purée through a sieve. On low heat, melt the butter and whisk in the purée. Froth with a hand stick blender to create froth.

7. To make the croutons, preheat the oven to 325°F. Melt the butter and toss in the bread cubes and finely chopped parsley. Bake for 10–15 minutes or until crunchy and toasted.

8. To serve the soup, return to heat and bring to a gentle boil. Lower the temperature and finish the soup by adding the cream. Taste to adjust the seasoning. Serve in individual bowls with a drizzle of frothy spring onion purée and a few herb croutons.

Shrimp in Garlic & Herb Butter with Crispy Breadcrumbs

Serves 6

Dublin Bay Prawns, known also by the French name "Langoustines" or by the name "Norway Lobsters," could be one of my favorite comfort foods from Ireland. They are a staple seafood in the colder waters of the north Atlantic, and though they were considered a delicacy to some, prawns were also a common food for many Irish people, particularly those who lived in coastal communities such as Dublin, Belfast, and Cork. The langoustines from Strangford Lough in County Down are considered some of the finest in the world.

Irish immigrants in America substituted Dublin Bay prawns for the more common, smaller pink or brown shrimp caught off the coast in North America, and today, most of the shrimp catch eaten in the United States comes from the Gulf of Mexico.

SHRIMP & TOPPING INGREDIENTS

32 large shrimp or Langoustine's (deveined with shells removed)
1½ cups of white sourdough breadcrumbs

GARLIC BUTTER INGREDIENTS

8 ounces (1 cup) salted butter
4 garlic cloves (crushed)
2 tablespoons parsley (chopped)
2 tablespoons chives (chopped)
Ground black pepper

HOW TO MAKE

1. Bring a pot of water to a boil and drop the shrimp in cooking just for a few minutes. The shrimp will float at the top when they are cooked, and the color will change from a pale opaque to a light pink color. Using a slotted spoon, drain and place in a bowl of ice water and then shell.

2. Preheat the oven to 375°F.

3. To make the garlic butter, beat the salted butter, garlic, chives, parsley, and freshly ground pepper by hand until the ingredients are all fully incorporated.

4. Divide the shrimp into 6 individual baking dishes for an appetizer or 4 dishes for a main course. Using the back of a knife spread the softened butter all over and then sprinkle with breadcrumbs.

5. Bake for 8–10 minutes until the breadcrumbs are golden brown and the garlic butter is sizzling.

6. Serve immediately with crusty white bread for sopping.

Beef & Oyster Irish Porter Pie

✍ *Serves 4–6* ✍

This classic Irish pie combines the best of Irish surf and turf, beef that calls to mind the cattle that have roamed the hills and green fields of Ireland for thousands of years, and salty oysters from the rocky shoreline of the wild Atlantic and the Irish Sea. These days, native oysters command big prices but there are some excellent sustainable farmed versions.

The cut of beef is an economical one which lends itself perfectly to the low, slow cooking method. It should be so tender; you should be able to be cut it with a spoon.

Both beef and oysters are combined here in hoppy gravy, thanks to our famous Irish porter, a perfect complement to its rich flavors. The succulent filling rests in a buttery puff pastry. And while the oysters are optional, I would say that the pie would not be complete without a pint of a dark Irish stout and a good story or two!

BEEF & OYSTER PIE INGREDIENTS

2¼ pounds of braising steak
1½ cups of onion (sliced)
2 tablespoons olive oil
2 slices of bacon (sliced thinly)
8 tablespoons butter
½ cup all-purpose flour
2 cups of Irish stout
1½ cups of beef stock
1 tablespoon sugar
1 teaspoon kosher salt
¼ teaspoon fresh ground black pepper
Bouquet garnet (thyme, rosemary, bay leaf tied together with string)
1 pound of shucked oysters (about 14–18)

PASTRY TOPPING INGREDIENTS

1 sheet of puff pastry (10–11-inch square)
1 egg (lightly beaten)
1 teaspoon of water

HOW TO MAKE

1. Heat the oil and butter in a large cooking pan and sear the meat on medium high heat working in small batches, browning on all sides. Add the onion and cook for 2–3 minutes to caramelize. Transfer the beef and onion to a bowl.

2. Reduce the heat to medium and add the bacon and cook until it is crispy and then transfer to the bowl with the beef.

3. Melt the butter and stir in the flour and cook for 2–3 minutes stirring to make a roux. Whisk in the Irish stout and the beef stock and bring to a simmer. Add the beef, onions, bacon, bouquet garnet and season with salt and pepper. Cover and bake for 2 hours until the beef is fork tender. Transfer into a deep pie dish.

4. Preheat the oven to 400°F.

5. Dry the shucked oysters on paper towels and stir into the beef and Irish stout.

6. Roll out the puff pastry on a lightly floured surface large enough to fit the dish. Cover the pie and score the pastry with a sharp knife and brush with beaten egg and water.

7. Bake for 25 minutes, or until the pastry is puffed and golden brown.

8. Serve immediately and enjoy!

Armagh Orchard Salad
with Apple Thyme Vinaigrette

꜒ *Serves 4–6* ꜖

In my home county of Armagh each year, residents eagerly await their fall apple harvest, the plump fruit hanging from the branches of thousands of apple trees dotting the county's landscape and country lanes. They give it its name, the Orchard County.

The dominant variety is the Armagh Bramley which has Protected Name Status. It was transplanted by an English lady in the 1920s and took hold. In recent years, much work has been done to reintroduce native varieties such as Dabinetts and Butchers Blood at the Apple Research Unit at Loughgall.

Apples are such a part of my childhood memories, and the memories of many other Irish immigrants from Mid-Ulster. The popularity of apples in the eastern United States would no doubt have been a great boost to many newly arrived Irish cooks.

This salad is my celebration of this beloved ingredient, and of harvest time when crisp autumn apples are so bountiful. Here, they come together with earthy toasted walnuts and tangy blue cheese, pairing perfectly with an herby apple dressing as a delicious starter or side dish.

A quick note here: green apples can be acidic, which is why I suggest the Pink Lady variety, paired with a creamier, less pungent blue cheese, such as Irish Cashel Blue. Cashel Blue farmhouse cheese is made from the milk of the Grubb's Friesian cows in County Tipperary, not too far away from the famous Rock of Cashel, an Irish landmark and icon of the culture for many.

SALAD INGREDIENTS

- 6 cups of greens (baby spinach and arugula mixed works very well)
- 1 Granny Smith green apple (hard cored removed and thinly sliced)
- 1 Pink Lady red apple (hard core removed and thinly sliced)
- ¾ cup of walnuts (chopped and toasted with 1 tablespoon of butter, kosher salt)
- 2 ounces (¼ cup) crumbled blue cheese

VINAIGRETTE INGREDIENTS

- 3 tablespoons apple cider vinegar
- 2 tablespoons cold pressed apple juice
- 2 tablespoons of honey
- 1 teaspoon of dry mustard powder
- 2 tablespoons shallot (finely chopped)
- ½ cup olive oil
- 2 teaspoons of fresh thyme leaves
- ½ teaspoons of sea salt
- ¼ teaspoon freshly cracked black pepper

HOW TO MAKE

1. Toast walnuts gently in a medium skillet over medium heat with butter and salt shaking gently for 2–5 minutes, or until they are golden brown and aromatic. Set aside to cool and chop.

2. To prepare the vinaigrette, add the apple cider vinegar, apple juice, honey, mustard, and shallot to a blender to combine and slowly drizzle in the olive oil. Add the thyme and season with salt and pepper. The ingredients can also be placed in a jar, sealed, and shaken together.

3. To assemble the salad, place the greens, chopped apples, blue cheese and nuts in a large bowl and toss in just about half of the vinaigrette before serving. Reserve some of the vinaigrette on the side, should your guests prefer to pour a little extra on their salad.

Dublin Coddle with Bangers & Bacon

Serves 4–6

Every culture has that one-pot dish that can be created easily with ingredients available in the pantry or fridge. In the case of an Irish kitchen, the family likely always has potatoes, onions, sausages, and bacon on hand, as those ingredients form the basis of many renowned Irish dishes.

They are also always available in Irish market towns, farmsteads, and shops. Irish butchers pride themselves on their particular sausage or bacon, and whilst many times these staples can be quite different in American stores, great options for traditional "bangers and bacon" can still normally be found.

It was a running joke in our family that our mother was such a good cook that she could make a gourmet meal out of a sausage, and a *coddle* was one such meal, a spontaneous dish she put together for our family as I was growing up.

I remember loving those simple, tasty suppers as we all sat around the farmhouse kitchen table. I have crafted my recipe here based on those memories, and it pairs wonderfully with a good cup of Irish tea.

CODDLE INGREDIENTS

1 tablespoon vegetable oil
4 slices of thick cut bacon (slice into ¼-inch strips)
1 pound (4–6) pork sausages (cut in thirds)
2 medium size red onions (sliced into strips)
2 cloves of garlic (sliced thinly)
1 tablespoon butter (room temperature)
1½ pounds potato (Yukon Golds or red skinned work great) thinly sliced
1¾ cups chicken stock
1½ tablespoons apple cider vinegar
Kosher salt and pepper
Handful fresh sage (olive oil to fry and course sea salt)

HOW TO MAKE

1. Heat the oil in a large skillet and fry bacon until crispy. Remove bacon from the skillet and set aside. Preheat the oven to 350°F.

2. Add the pork sausages to the skillet and brown on all sides. Remove the sausages from the pan and set aside.

3. Pour all but 2 tablespoons of oil from the skillet and fry the red onions until they are caramelized. Add the garlic and cook for 1 minute. Deglaze the pan with the apple cider vinegar and chicken stock scraping down all the brown bits and reduce for a few minutes.

4. Grease a 9 x 13-inch dish with butter and then layer the potatoes, seasoning with salt and pepper on each layer. Sprinkle the onion and garlic over it. Spoon sausages on top. Pour the stock over the dish.

5. Bake in oven for 50 minutes until the potatoes are soft and most of the liquid has evaporated.

6. For garnish, first fry the sage leaves in a little olive oil for just a few seconds and sprinkle them with sea salt. Sprinkle the fried sage over the reserved bacon, then transfer the mix to the oven for a few minutes to let it warm.

Loin of Bacon with Crispy Cabbage & Mustard Sauce

Serves 4–6

In the United States, corn beef and cabbage has earned its place as the noble national Irish dish, especially on St. Patrick's Day, but it is not actually very well known in Ireland itself.

If you ask any Irish immigrant about corn beef and cabbage, they will happily share that while they do enjoy corn beef, slow-cooked bacon loin is closer to the food they remember from Ireland. The recipe is an old favorite, normally paired with cabbage and cooked in a skillet.

While American bacon is made from the pork belly, Irish bacon is more like Canadian bacon in that it comes from the back of the pig. Irish bacon is typically cut into a round shape with a little fat left on the outside. It is also meaty, salty, and delicious.

I encourage you to get to know the more authentic version of this Irish dish—one that is quick, tasty, and impossible not to enjoy. If you really want to get into the mood, search for the Irish country singer Brendan Shine's iconic song "I'm a Savage for Bacon and Cabbage."

BACON INGREDIENTS

3 pounds cured loin of bacon
2 bay leaves
1 teaspoon peppercorns
1 stick of celery (chopped)
1 large onion (cut in quarters)
1 carrot (chopped)

CABBAGE INGREDIENTS

1 large green savoy cabbage (hard core removed and thinly sliced)
3 tablespoons of butter
2 tablespoons water
Kosher salt and freshly ground black pepper

MUSTARD CREAM SAUCE

3 tablespoons butter
2 tablespoons all-purpose flour
½ cup heavy whipping cream
½ cup reserved cooking liquid
1 tablespoon whole grain mustard

HOW TO MAKE

1. Put the bacon in a large saucepan and cover with cold water. Add the bay leaves, peppercorns, celery, and carrot. Bring to the boil and then cover with a lid and reduce the heat to a low simmer for 20 minutes per pound plus an additional 30 minutes.

2. Remove the bacon from the pan and set aside. Reserve ½ cup of cooking liquid for the sauce.

3. To make the mustard sauce, melt the butter and add the flour cooking for a minute and then whisk in the reserved cooking liquid, heavy whipping cream, mustard and salt and pepper. Taste to adjust seasonings!

4. To make the cabbage, melt the butter in a large skillet and then add the cabbage tossing with tongs until it looks bright and smells fragrant. Sprinkle 2 tablespoons of water over the cabbage to wilt slightly but remaining crispy and bright.

5. To serve slice the bacon and drizzle with a little mustard sauce and top with crispy cabbage.

Cullen Skink Seafood Bake

❧ *Serves 4–6* ☙

A traditional Celtic fish pie made with smoked haddock, there are several variations of this dish—including a pie or as a thick, hearty soup—across Scotland and Ireland. The strange, whimsical name has two origins: the town of Cullen in the northeast of Scotland, and the Scots word '*skink*' which described a *shin*, or the basis of a soup.

Here, flaky haddock is baked in a white cheese sauce made from the poached fish stock. The pie is then topped with buttery mashed potato and a crunchy golden topping of firm Irish cheese. Very hearty and very tasty.

This pie was a tradition in our house every Friday when the local markets were stocked with the freshest seafood. It is a recipe that has been passed down through our family for many generations, and cooking and tasting this wonderful dish always takes me home.

SEAFOOD BASE INGREDIENTS

1½ cups of milk
1½ cups cold water
1 small bay leaf
6 peppercorns
1 small onion (peeled and sliced)
1½ pounds smoked haddock (skinless and boneless)
8 ounces raw prawns (peeled)

PARSLEY INGREDIENTS

3 tablespoons butter
3 tablespoons of all-purpose flour
1 teaspoon lemon juice
2 tablespoons parsley (chopped)

POTATO LAYER INGREDIENTS

1 pound potatoes (peeled and cut)
4 tablespoons of butter
¼ cup warm milk

TOPPING INGREDIENTS

¼ cup breadcrumbs
½ cup Irish cheddar cheese (grated)

HOW TO MAKE

1. Place the haddock and prawns in a pan with the milk, water, bay leaf, peppercorn, and onion. Season with salt and pepper and slowly poach for 8–10 minutes (reserve 2 cups of stock).

2. While the fish is poaching, prepare potato topping by boiling the potatoes in a pot of cold salted water for 20 minutes.

3. To make the sauce, melt the butter in a small saucepan and stir in the flour cooking for one minute and then whisk in 2 cups of reserved stock and lemon juice and bring to a simmer. Stir in the parsley and season with a little salt and pepper.

4. Strain water from the potatoes, then place back on to the heat for a few minutes to remove excess moisture. Mash the potatoes with the warm milk and butter. Season with salt and pepper and stir in the Dubliner Irish cheese.

5. Preheat the oven to 375°F.

6. To assemble, pour the parsley sauce over the seafood, spoon on the potato and finally sprinkle the bread-crumbs and cheese topping over the top. Bake for 20 minutes and serve right away.

Emerald Ulster Potato Champ

Serves 4–6

Champ is a staple potato dish from the northern province of Ulster, where I grew up. My grandmother would often make her champ with stinging nettles and scallions in the old-fashioned Irish style. Stinging nettles grow wild throughout Ireland and are considered a foe rather than friend to many because of their stinging leaves—which can leave a nasty rash should you fall into them, something I often did as a child!

Nettle leaves can only be used in the springtime when they are delicate, and Irish people took particular care when picking them. The cooking process removes the sting, leaving only a tasty, nutritious ingredient behind.

My family traditionally served our champ as a large dollop in the center of the plate with a well in the middle, into which we placed a large scoop of Irish creamery butter. In my new twist on this classic dish, I fold in the cheese and purée the spring onions, and nettles or spinach, so that the potatoes will be a vibrant green color when folded in.

I make this every year for St. Patrick's Day, when it's our time to go green, and I hope you enjoy!

POTATO CHAMP INGREDIENTS

2½ pounds potatoes (floury variety such as Idaho)
Several handfuls of nettle tops (or substitute spinach leaves)
1 bunch (1 cup) green onions (chopped)
4 fluid ounces (½ cup) heavy whipping cream
4 fluid ounces (½ cup) milk
4 fluid ounces (½ cup) Irish butter
1 teaspoon sea salt
½ teaspoon ground black pepper
4 ounces (1 cup) aged cheddar cheese

HOW TO MAKE

1. Peel and quarter potatoes. Place them in a large pan and cook in enough cold water to cover the potatoes for 30 minutes or until tender.

2. Drain the potatoes, cover the pan, and allow them to dry for a few minutes.

3. While the potatoes are still cooking, combine 2 ounces of butter, the heavy whipping cream, and milk, bringing them to a boil.

4. Blanch one bunch (1 cup) of green onions with the nettle leaves in a pan of boiling water allowing them to simmer for 2–3 minutes, and then quickly transfer them to a bowl of ice water to keep a vibrant green color.

5. Purée the green onions and nettles together in a food processor. Slowly combine the heated heavy cream, milk, and melted butter to the green onion purée.

6. Run the cooked potatoes through a ricer or food mill and then fold in the green onion purée mixture to make a smooth consistency. Stir in the cheddar cheese.

7. Serve in a warm serving bowl, making a shallow hole in the center of the potatoes with the back of a spoon. Fill with the remaining 2 ounces of melted butter and serve immediately.

Lough Erne Boxty
with Cheese & Chives

◝ *Serves 4–6* ◞

Boxty hails from the north midlands of Ireland. It is particularly associated with the border counties Longford, Cavan, Louth, and Fermanagh.

The name Boxty comes from the Irish *aran bocht ti*, meaning "poor house bread." It is made from simple ingredients that would have likely been available to most Irish people, regardless of their station in life: finely grated potato, flour, baking soda, salt, and milk. My favorite way to enjoy a boxty is as a wonderful base for smoked salmon, or as part of a hearty Irish breakfast.

If you have been to Temple Bar in Dublin, you will more than likely have eaten in Gallagher's Boxty House. Indeed, in recent years, there has been a resurgence in boxty's popularity with artisan versions appearing on supermarket shelves nationwide. Apparently, it is naturally low in fat, but it is hard not to slather it in butter!

My dear friend Noel McMeel, Executive Head Chef at Lough Erne Resorts, comes from the border county of Fermanagh. I asked him if he would share with me his regional family recipe, going back many generations. He has kindly offered it here, scrumptious, and simple.

BOXTY INGREDIENTS

2 large floury variety potatoes (such as Idaho or Russets peeled)
½ teaspoon baking powder
½ teaspoon salt
1 cup cooked mashed potatoes
1 egg (beaten)
1 cup all-purpose flour (plus 1 tablespoon for dusting)
½ cup grated Irish Cheddar Cheese
¼ cup chives (finely snipped)
6–8 tablespoon milk or buttermilk (enough to make an even consistency)
3 tablespoons salted Irish butter

HOW TO MAKE

1. To make the Boxty cakes, peel the potatoes and then finely grate into clean bowl. Next spoon the potatoes into a clean towel or cheesecloth and strain the subsequent liquid into the bowl. Discard any of the clear liquid but keep the remaining starch to add to the cakes.

2. Stir in the baking powder and salt and pepper to the grated potatoes. When mixed, add the cool mashed potato, egg, flour, grated cheese, reserved starch, and enough milk to make an even dropping consistency. The cakes should be about ½-inch thick and drop easily on to the pan.

3. Heat a skillet to medium high heat and add the salted butter. Portion the dough out into four even portions and sauté for 3–4 minutes on each side until potatoes are fully cooked.

Zesty Lemon Posset

The Irish have always loved creating desserts made with cream because of the abundance of farm fresh milk cream available throughout the island. *Posset* is one such dessert, a very old-style dish where the cream is sometimes spiced and curdled with ale. In Ireland, as far back as medieval times, possets were also flavored with honey, and this version substitutes the spice or ale for a zesty lemon flavor.

Serving delicate lemon posset for dessert has been a tradition on special occasions in my family for many generations. Our version has a decadent, velvety texture, and is best enjoyed chilled. Seasonal berries, such as blackberries or raspberries, are also a colorful and delicious addition when serving this dreamy, creamy dessert.

Your lemon posset will keep for three days when stored in the refrigerator. And a little goes a long way because of the richness of the cream, but it is well worth every bite.

POSSET INGREDIENTS

2 cups (1 pint) heavy cream
2 lemons (5 tablespoons plus zest)
⅔ cup fine granulated sugar

GARNISH INGREDIENTS

8 blackberries/raspberries
Edible flower petals (optional)

HOW TO MAKE

1. Finely grate the zest of lemons and then juice.

2. In a small saucepan heat the cream, sugar and lemon zest to a gentle boil stirring for 8–12 minutes until the sugar has dissolved and the cream has reduced slightly.

3. Remove the saucepan from the heat and whisk in the lemon juice.

4. Allow the posset to cool slightly for at least 20 minutes or so, before pouring into containers (4 martini glasses or 8 shot glasses). It is advised to strain the posset mixture to remove any zest or skin that has formed.

5. Refrigerate for at least 2 hours until they have set.

6. Before serving garnish with a fresh berry and optional edible flower petals.

NOTE: Serves 4 when poured in martini glasses or 8 in mini shot glasses.

Oaty Bramley Apple Crumble with Pouring Cream

Serves 4

Growing up amongst the orchards of Mid Ulster, there was never a family gathering where we did not have apple crumbles or pies with cream on the table.

Generations of Irish people have loved Bramley's, and they can only be classified as true Armagh Bramley apples if they are grown in their specific region of Ireland. The harsh, cold, windy weather of the island gives them their unique tart and tangy flavor.

The closest apple I have found to the Bramley's here are Granny Smith apples, and countless Irish immigrants have no doubt made the same substitution when cooking, just as I did when I landed in America. I have substituted Granny Smiths in this recipe, and it can also be made as a gluten-free dessert if you substitute gluten-free oats.

A traditional crumble is one of my favorite food memories from childhood, and this one takes me back to my family's kitchen table. I hope it finds a home on yours.

CRUMPLE INGREDIENTS

6 Granny Smith apples (peeled and diced)
½ vanilla pod (split in half and seeds scraped out)
4 ounces (½ cup) fine granulated sugar
2 tablespoons butter
1 tablespoon lemon juice
1 tablespoon honey

TOPPING INGREDIENTS

3 ounces (1 cup) rolled oats (use gluten free oats if preferred)
1½ ounces (½ cup) almond flour
2 ounces (¼ cup) unsalted butter
2 ounces (¼ cup) light brown sugar
1 ounce sliced almonds

SERVE WITH

¼ cup of light cream

HOW TO MAKE

1. Toss the apples with the sugar and the vanilla seeds.

2. Melt the butter in the pan and add the apples, cook for 7–8 minutes until they begin to break down but are not too soft. Add the lemon and honey.

3. Transfer the apple filling into small ramekin dishes.

4. Preheat the oven to 350°F.

5. To make the topping, place the almond flour and oats in the food processor and whizz to break down the oats a little. Add the sugar and then the butter until it resembles breadcrumbs. Stir in the sliced almonds.

6. Sprinkle the crumble mixture over the apple mixture.

7. Place the ramekins on a baking tray and bake for about 18 minutes or until the crumble topping is golden brown and the fruit is bubbling.

8. Delicious served with chilled pouring cream or vanilla ice cream (your choice)!

IRISH IMMIGRANT FOODS

Chapter Two

My Heart Finds a Home

Irish food to comfort the soul, settling in a new land

For many immigrants, the first few weeks and months in a new land are crucial. When my husband and I moved to America from Ireland in 1996, we had a job waiting for us, we had some resources and an airline waiting to fly us home if things did not work out. Not so for Etta and John a century before. For most Irish immigrants, the journey to America was long, hard, and taken only once. They typically never returned to Ireland, resigning their homeland to a quiet, locked place in their memory.

Settling In and Settling Down

Etta sailed to Boston in 1896, a year before tall ships were replaced by new steamers. Her journey likely took many days and nights, requiring her to sleep and live on the boat in cramped conditions. I imagine her eagerly anticipating her arrival, gazing at the bright stars hanging above a vast, black ocean, dreaming of what may come. She was twenty-one years old and sailing into the great unknown.

In those days, immigrants passed through a clearance house as they disembarked from their ships, a disorienting experience undertaken before walking through the doors at the end of the shed, out into the bright light that was opportunity in America.

Etta was particularly fortunate; she disembarked in the States with a possible job already lined up—an interview for a lady's maid position in the home of an established Massachusetts family in the coastal town of Plymouth, arranged by her older sister.

The lady of that house, Mrs. Woods, met Etta during a visit to Boston. Etta was a young Irish girl, pretty and elegant, respectful, and eager to learn. I imagine Mrs. Woods liked Etta at once, as she accompanied Mrs. Woods immediately back to her substantial house on the coast.

Etta was one of three maids serving this family, and by all accounts, she rose to the occasion. My mother remembers her grandmother's impeccable manners and grace–characteristics no doubt instilled in her

during Etta's service in the Woods' grand house in New England, with all of its pomp and circumstance, silver teapots, linen and lace.

One year later, John would also disembark in America. He did not have a job lined up like Etta, but he was a talented worker, strong and good with his hands.

After arriving in the United States, John spent several days in immigrant lodging. It was recommended to him there to try his luck in Brookline, a community characterized by beautiful homes and wealthy families who were often in need of strong, skilled laborers. Establishing himself in this suburb, John worked on building sites and as a gardener, putting to use the skills he learned on his 30 acres in the shadow of the Mourne Mountains in County Down.

John slowly gained a reputation as a talented carpenter. He purchased his own tools and took on his own jobs for wealthy New England families, saving his earnings along the way. After one such job in Brookline, he was recommended to the Woods family from Plymouth. They were in need of a skilled carpenter to work on their home. Though it was quite a distance to travel, John had an adventurous spirit and so took the job.

Little did he know that the Woods also employed a young Irish lady's maid, a girl of grace and strength, who would change the course of his life forever.

Like John and Etta, all immigrants confront the challenges of learning to feel at home in their new land. There are new ways of doing things, a new culture to understand, and of course, new foods to explore.

My husband and I moved from Ireland to New England in 1996, and shortly thereafter to Atlanta and the Deep South. While I learned to embrace the new foods of these new lands and cultures, my Irish heart still longed for everything that was home. I missed my family; I missed the beauty of the Irish landscape. I missed the close-knit community and the traditions of my native land, so I poured that longing into the embrace of Irish comfort foods. Like the millions of immigrants before me, finding a taste of home in a newly adopted land can be a challenge, but walk with me as I introduce you to some of my favorite comfort food recipes that I enjoyed, and I know you will, too!

CHAPTER TWO

Irish Comfort Foods

Sunday Supper Rosemary Chicken Supreme
(page 57)

Earthy Celeriac & Apple Soup

Soups are the ultimate comfort food for Irish immigrants, especially during the rainy, cold winter months that remind us of our homeland.

Hearth cooking in old Ireland, the method by which our soups are often prepared, would have included a pot around an open fire, full of soup to share with family and hospitable strangers alike. My grandmother would often add more stock to her soups if she needed to make them stretch to feed more hungry bellies.

I can imagine early immigrants, even those before my great grandmother's time, craving soul-warming bowls of soup to cheer their tired hearts in the New World.

I am a huge fan of the versatility of soups, as well. For this recipe, it is the combination of green apples and celery root, with their dual sweet and savory notes. Celeriac is not the prettiest root vegetable to look at, but it has a beautiful, unique nutty flavor, and a smooth, creamy texture works that works perfectly in soups—they are also a great, low-carb mash substitute for potatoes.

I love to serve this soup at elegant dinner parties in between courses, as the flavors are exceptionally clean and palate cleansing.

SOUP INGREDIENTS

2 tablespoons butter
2 medium (1½ cups) Vidalia onions (chopped)
1 celeriac, peeled and diced
2 medium (1½ cups) Granny Smith apples (peeled and chopped)
4 cups chicken stock
2 cups freshly pressed apple juice
1 teaspoon sea salt
½ teaspoon freshly ground black pepper
1 teaspoon curry powder

GARNISH INGREDIENTS

3 ounces apple wood smoked bacon (cooked to crispy and chopped)
½ Granny Smith apple (cut into matchsticks)
2 tablespoons crème fraiche
Squeeze of lemon juice
Pinch of salt

HOW TO MAKE

1. In a large soup pot, melt the butter and sauté the onions, celeriac, and apple over a medium to low heat, then cover and cook until they are beginning to color for another 8–10 minutes, stirring occasionally.

2. Add the stock, apple juice, curry powder and salt and pepper and simmer for 25 minutes until all the ingredients are tender and the liquid has slightly reduced. Taste to adjust seasoning.

3. Using a hand blender, purée the soup until smooth or use a food processor.

4. To serve, place 1 teaspoon of chopped bacon and apple in each warm bowl. Combine crème fraiche, lemon juice and salt, and swirl a little over each soup bowl.

Crispy Shallot Topped Greens with Warm Bacon Vinaigrette

A well-worn cast iron skillet has been the cherished possession of many an Irish cook, often handed down, generation to generation. Families in Ireland often talk about *"getting the pan on,"* and all Irish immigrants crave those tasty, crispy, fried foods that remind us of our home kitchens. *"Getting the pan on"* could have meant anything from frying meats, eggs, and potatoes to breads for what we call "a fry up."

In this recipe, we use the cast iron skillet for crisping up bacon with garlic and shallots, the perfect crunchy accoutrements for turning a bright, light salad into a filling comfort food. Shallots have a more delicate, sweet flavor, as opposed to the intense bite you get with an onion. For this dish, the garlic and shallots are best cut using a mandolin.

When paired with light, bright spring greens, the crispy, crunchy bacon garnish included in this recipe leaves you feeling satisfied, minus the guilt! It is a wonderful comfort dish, one that I have always enjoyed and I hope you will, too!

SALAD GREENS INGREDIENTS

2½ ounces (5 cups) organic spring greens

DRESSING INGREDIENTS

1 tablespoon vegetable oil
5 slices uncured applewood smoked bacon (finely chopped)
8 tablespoons (½ cup) olive oil
3 garlic cloves (finely sliced)
¼ cup white balsamic vinegar
1 teaspoon Dijon mustard
1 teaspoon sugar
Freshly ground black pepper

FRIED SHALLOTS INGREDIENTS

2 shallots (finely sliced)
1 tablespoon flour
1 cup vegetable oil
Kosher salt and pepper

HOW TO MAKE

1. Heat the oil in skillet and crisp bacon. Remove bacon from the pan and set on plate lined with a paper towel. Drain bacon fat from skillet leaving 1 tablespoon for a little flavor.

2. Add the slivered garlic and cook for 1 minute to soften but not brown. Remove from heat and add vinegar (being careful as pan may splutter some). Gently shake the saucepan to mix. Use as whisk to mix the mustard, sugar. Add ground black pepper. Finally whisk in the olive oil and gently heat on low.

3. Toss the sliced shallots in flour. Heat the oil in a medium saucepan or fryer to 360°F. Add the shallots in small batches so they do not stick together cooking for 10–12 minutes until they are crispy. Remove with a slotted spoon and place on paper towels to drain. Season the shallots with a little salt and pepper.

4. To serve, toss the greens in the warm vinaigrette with the bacon.

5. Serve right away and top each salad serving with a small handful of fried shallots and enjoy!

'Cead Mìle Fàilte' Kale Dip

Serves 4

To ease their lonely hearts, early Irish immigrants often lived near one another, making it easy to gather in community. They soon became known for their sense of warm welcome and fun spirit, and in turn were able to integrate quickly into the cultural melting pot of the New World. They established their reputation for festive parties, complete with dancing, singing, storytelling, and of course, delicious food.

For our family gatherings and parties, I often turn to this delectable dip, one of our favorites for all kinds of occasions. The smell of that bubbling cheese is a lovely Cead Mile Failte, the Gaelic phrase for *"one hundred thousand welcomes."*

This appetizer is served piping hot from the oven, and is a true crowd-pleaser, welcoming everyone into the kitchen. Shared appetizers encourage guests to mix and mingle, breaking the ice and getting the party going Irish style!

KALE DIP INGREDIENTS

6 ounces of lacinato kale (1 bunch with the stems removed and roughly chopped)
12 ounces artichoke hearts (frozen or canned, drained/chopped)
½ cup plain Greek yogurt
1 cup mayonnaise
2 tablespoons whole grain mustard
3 garlic cloves (minced)
1 teaspoon kosher salt
¼ teaspoon fresh ground pepper
2 cups mature cheddar cheese (grated)
1 tablespoon butter (room temperature)
Dash of hot sauce

TOPPING INGREDIENTS

¼ cup of cheddar cheese
¼ cup of panko breadcrumbs

SERVING INGREDIENTS

Vegetable crudités (cucumber, radish, carrot, celery)
Garlic toasts

HOW TO MAKE

1. Bring a large saucepan of water to a boil and blanch the kale for 30 seconds to slightly wilt and then quickly remove, strain, and set it aside. When the kale has cooled, chop it slightly.

2. Preheat the oven to 375°F.

3. Combine the yogurt, mayo, mustard, hot sauce, garlic, salt, pepper, cheese and finally fold in the prepared kale and chopped artichokes.

4. Grease an 8-inch oven proof dish with butter and then spoon in the resulting dip.

5. Bake the dip for 18–20 minutes until the dip is bubbling and has a golden-brown crust.

6. Serve with garlic toasts and vegetable crudités.

Spiced Parsnip, Pear & Ginger Soup

Root vegetables grow particularly well in the dark, fertile soils of Ireland, and guests who visit constantly rave about the warm bowls of puréed root vegetable soups they enjoy in our pubs and restaurants. Creamy, savory and slightly sweet, this soup, flavored with spiced parsnip, pear, and ginger, is one of my favorite combinations for a celebratory occasion. The parsnips' nutty flavor compliments the floral sweetness of pears spiced with fresh ginger to wonderful effect.

A high quality smoked oil is also important for bringing out the flavors of this recipe. Each year when I return to America from Ireland, I make sure to steal away some precious bottles of rapeseed oil, including the award-winning Broighter Gold oil from Limavady, and from the Twelve Hotel in Galway, who smoke their oil producing an incredible flavor note.

If you happen to visit Ireland in the early summer, look out for the beautiful fields of golden rapeseed flowers, which in turn produce that superb golden oil so prized by Irish cooks, and so perfect for dishes such as this one.

SOUP INGREDIENTS

2 tablespoons butter/olive oil
1 medium onion (1 cup chopped)
1 celery stick (¾ cup diced)
5 parsnips (4 cups peeled and diced)
4 medium ripe pears (3 cups of Bosc or d'Anjou peeled and chopped)
2 teaspoons grated fresh ginger
6 cups vegetable stock
2 cups water
1 teaspoon sea salt
½ teaspoon freshly ground black pepper
2 teaspoons curry powder

GARNISH INGREDIENTS

½ pear (cut into matchsticks)
Squeeze of lemon juice
Drizzle of good smoked oil (Irish rapeseed or olive oil)

HOW TO MAKE

1. In a large soup pot, melt the butter and sauté the onions, celery, parsnips, pears and grated fresh ginger over a medium to low heat, then cover and cook until they are fragrant and beginning to color for 5 minutes, stirring occasionally.

2. Add the stock, water, curry powder and salt and pepper and simmer for 25 minutes until all the ingredients are tender and the liquid has slightly reduced. Taste to adjust seasoning.

3. Using a hand blender, purée the soup until smooth or use a food processor to purée the soup in batches until smooth.

4. To serve, place about 1 tablespoon of chopped pear in each warm bowl followed by the soup and then drizzle with a little smoked oil.

Inis Mor Aran Island Goat Cheese Soufflés

SOUFFLE INGREDIENTS

The women in my family tree are *all* great cooks and were renowned for taking quite simple ingredients that were available in rural Ireland and turning them into incredible dishes, like soufflés. Soufflés may sound fancy, but in fact, they are simply light, puffy cakes made with egg yolks and beaten egg whites. An inexpensive dish that the talented, resourceful cooks in my family have returned to again and again.

This recipe is divine, especially when made in Ireland with award-winning goat cheese from the largest of the Aran Islands, Inis Mor. What makes Inis Mor cheese so special? The goats that the cheese comes from get to graze on 250 varieties of wild grasses, herbs, and thistles that grow on the islands. The grasses are ancient and wild, and as a result, the cheese is splendid! Irish cheese producers also know that the natural sea breezes of the islands contribute to a natural saltiness in the dairy, a flavor and experience that has to be tasted to be believed!

Owner Gabriel Faherty was a deep-sea fisher-man who started making goat cheese about ten years ago. Aran Goats' Cheese is the only Econo-musee on an island in Ireland. It is a must visit, meet the goats whose milk makes the cheese and try some of the brilliantly named Paramasaran, the Gouda or the Feta-style.

A soufflé is a lovely way to enjoy the pure flavor of local goat cheese, wherever you find it, and are great sources of comfort, indeed. Even better—this twice-baked recipe allows you to make them ahead of time for easy entertaining! Enjoy!

3 tablespoons (1½ ounces) unsalted butter (plus more for greasing ramekins)
8 ounces (1 cup) whole milk
Small piece of onion
6 whole pink peppercorns
Sprig of thyme
1 bay leaf
Pinch of salt
6 tablespoons (1½ ounces) flour
6 ounces goat cheese
4 eggs (separated)
¾ cup heavy whipping cream

HOW TO MAKE

1. Preheat oven to 375°F. Butter 6 ramekin dishes and prepare baking pan for bain-marie (pan must be at least 2-inches deep).

2. In a medium size saucepan warm milk, onion, peppercorns, thyme, and bay leaf and infuse for 10 minutes. Strain liquid into a small bowl and discard everything else.

3. Prepare béchamel sauce by melting butter in a clean heavy based saucepan. Add the flour and cook for 1–2 minutes until it becomes a glossy, smooth paste (being careful not to brown). Whisk in the warmed milk a little at a time and stir until sauce thickens and comes to a gentle boil. Cook for 2 minutes and remove from heat. Stir in 4 ounces of the goat cheese. Beat in egg yolks one at a time.

4. In a heavy-duty mixer beat eggs whites until foamy. To lighten the soufflés, stir in a little of the egg white mixture and then fold the remaining using a large metal spoon.

5. Fill buttered ramekin dishes. Place them in a prepared pan and fill with boiling water from kettle at least ½-inch deep. Bake for 20 minutes and then transfer to a cooling rack to cool slightly. Turn out each soufflé upside down into a large, buttered baking dish. Cover and refrigerate for up to 24 hours.

6. To reheat the soufflés, bring to room temperature. Preheat oven to 375 degrees. Sprinkle remaining 2 ounces of goat cheese on top of each one and then bake for 15 minutes until lightly browned and puffed up. Spoon cream over soufflés and bake for 5 more minutes.

7. We recommend you serve this with our mixed organic green salad with garlic bacon vinaigrette.

Monday, the Meatless Shepherd's Pie

❧ *Serves 4–6* ☙

Ground beef or lamb cooked with a topping of mashed potatoes is known as cottage or shepherd's pie, and this most famous dish was brought over to the New World by Irish, Scots, and English immigrants. It is thought that these savory, homey pies were invented as a resourceful way to use left-overs from the Sunday roast, ensuring no meat was wasted. Our family decided to implement a weekly 'Meatless Monday' several years ago to incorporate more plant-based foods, such as vegetables, beans, and nuts. Noble idea, but I still longed for the comforting, meaty, Irish farmhouse foods I grew up on. That longing led to the creation of my meatless version of famous shepherd's pie. The combination of lentils and mushrooms are one of my favorite meat substitutes, as they are flavorful and have a natural, hearty texture. The mash topping can be made from white potatoes, celeriac, sweet potatoes, turnips, rutabaga, or my favorite parsnip, carrots, and white potatoes combination. Feel free to top with your favorite root vegetable mash and enjoy.

VEGETABLE BASE INGREDIENTS

4-6 tablespoons of butter (olive oil or coconut oil can be substituted)
8 ounces mushrooms (chopped)
2 cups onions (2 medium size, chopped)
3 cloves of garlic (crushed)
1 cup celery (2-3 ribs, finely chopped)
1 teaspoon of dried thyme (chopped)
1 teaspoon of dried rosemary (chopped)
1 bay leaf
¼ cup of tomato paste
2 teaspoons sugar
2½ cups (16 ounces) of green lentils
7 cups of vegetable broth
2 tablespoons soy sauce/liquid aminos
2 teaspoons of salt
¼ teaspoon white pepper

MASH TOPPING INGREDIENTS

2 pounds of celeriac/parsnips/carrots (equal parts, peeled and cut in to 1-inch chunks)
1 teaspoon salt (plus extra to salt the water for cooking)
½ cup of Greek yogurt
¼ cup of melted butter (or substitute with olive oil)
1 tablespoon parsley (chopped)

HOW TO MAKE

1. To make the vegetable base, heat 3–4 tablespoons of butter in a large skillet over medium high heat. Add the mushrooms in a single layer and cook them undisturbed until the bottom side is golden brown. Season with salt and pepper, toss, and turn them over to let continue to brown on both sides. Transfer to a separate bowl. In the same saucepan, add the remaining oil and add the onion to the pan and cook until they are translucent. Add the chopped celery and garlic and cook until they are fragrant.

2. Add the lentils, stock, tomato paste, sugar, soy sauce, thyme and bay leaf and simmer slowly for 45 minutes or until the lentils are soft. Add back the mushrooms, season with salt and pepper and remove the bay leaf.

3. To make the topping, peel the carrots, parsnips and celeriac and cut into small pieces. Place in a large pot of cold salted water and bring to a boil. Cook the root vegetables until for about 20–25 minutes, or until they are fork tender and drain, placing back on the heat to dry out a little before mashing and mixing in the Greek yogurt and melted butter. Taste to adjust seasoning.

4. Preheat the oven to 350°F.

5. To assemble the pie, lightly grease a 9 x 13-inch pan. Spoon the vegetable base into the pan and then spread the celeriac, carrot, and parsnip topping, fluffing with a fork. Bake for 30–40 minutes or until the pie is bubbling. Sprinkle a little fresh parsley on top and serve.

Lamb Chops & Leeks with Sausage Skirlie

"Skirlie" is a traditional, Old-World Scottish recipe made with oatmeal, and fried in creamery butter, onions, and herbs. The word "skirlie" comes from the sizzling, clicking noise made by the ingredients frying in the skillet as all the tasty elements come together.

I can recall my grandmother serving me "skirlie mash" in typical Irish style with potatoes, as a simple supper dish. Nutty, toasted steel-cut oatmeal offers a taste of home comfort, as many an Irish immigrant likely longed for skirl after a long, cold New England winter day.

Skirlie is a delicious complement to lamb chops, and the more modern addition of peppery hot Chorizo sausage gives this old Scotch Irish dish a modern twist!

LAMB INGREDIENTS

3 pounds (8-12 bone) rack of lamb, trimmed
2 tablespoons olive oil

MARINADE INGREDIENTS

2 tablespoons lemon juice
1 teaspoon lemon zest
1 tablespoon olive oil
1 tablespoon rosemary (chopped)
2 cloves of garlic (minced)
½ teaspoon salt
¼ teaspoon fresh ground black pepper

JUS INGREDIENTS

½ cup vegetable stock
¼ cup red wine

CHORIZO & LEEK SKIRLIE

2-3 tablespoons vegetable oil
4 ounces Chorizo sausage (casing removed and diced)
8 ounces leeks (washed and chopped)
8 ounces quick cooking steel cut oatmeal
4-6 ounces of chicken stock
Salt and freshly ground pepper

HOW TO MAKE

1. Combine marinade ingredients together and rub over rack of lamb. Cover and refrigerate for at least 30 minutes.

2. Remove lamb from marinate and season with sea salt and freshly milled black pepper.

3. Preheat oven to 425°F. Heat olive oil in a heavy based skillet over high heat. Sear the rack of lamb for 2–3 minutes on each side.

4. Place rack of lamb bone side down on the skillet and place in preheated oven. Roast in oven for 1–12 minutes for medium well done and for 15 minutes for well done. Cover and rest for 7–9 minutes prior to slicing.

5. To make skirlie, heat the vegetable oil in a large skillet. Add the Chorizo and cook for 2–3 minutes. Add the chopped leeks and cook for 2 minutes to soften. Stir in the oatmeal and cook for 5–6 minutes. Add the chicken stock and cook for a few more minutes until all the moisture has evaporated. Season with salt and pepper.

6. Remove lamb from the skillet and slice rack of lamb between the ribs. Deglaze the skillet with a little stock and red wine and cook to reduce slightly.

7. To serve, spoon a little skirlie in the center of the plate. Top with 2–3 chops per person and drizzle with a little jus.

Thyme-Poached Leeks in a Rich Cheese Sauce

Serves 4–6

Creamy leeks are true Irish soul food, a food of the common man, and have been grown in Ireland for many generations. Roy Lyttle's leeks grown on the Ards Peninsula are among the sweetest you will taste. They benefit from the area's unique micro-climate, but any leeks braised in the way of this recipe will certainly earn their keep.

The Irish brought to America the idea of combining ham or bacon with these leeks, as well as cabbage and potatoes, spawning a full array of leek-inspired dishes. And this particular dish is one of my very favorites.

The rolling green fields of County Armagh where I grew up are lush, fertile, and nutrient-rich. The farm beside ours grew leeks, as well as carrots, parsnips, and potatoes, and they were always glad to share with their fellow neighbors in a non-spoken honors system.

When we were gifted a new delivery of freshly dug leeks, my mother didn't waste any time incorporating them into our daily menu. Sunday lunch was always a special affair in our family, when we would cook a roasted meat, worthy of a decadent and comforting side of leeks in a rich cheese sauce, just like this one.

POACHED LEEKS INGREDIENTS

4 large leeks or 8 medium (cleaned under running water)
Small bunch of thyme
1¾ cups heavy cream
1 garlic clove (cut in half)
2 ounces (¼ cup) of grated gruyere cheese
Sea salt
Freshly ground pepper
Butter for greasing dish

HOW TO MAKE

1. Preheat the oven to 400°F.

2. Use a sharp knife to cut off the tough outer green parts of the leeks leaving all the white and the lighter green parts. Wash the leeks. (I like to make a large slit through the leek leaving the root intact and clean under running water.) Cut the leeks into halves length wise and then slice in to larger 2-inch size pieces.

3. Place the leeks into a large saucepan with the thyme and cover with the heavy whipping cream. Season with salt and pepper and bring to a low simmer and cook for 15–18 minutes until the leeks are tender.

4. Butter a shallow baking dish and smear the garlic clove around for just a hint of flavor.

5. Transfer the leeks to the baking dish and pour the cream on top. Discard the thyme. Sprinkle with the grated cheese and bake for 10 minutes until the dish is bubbling and the cheese has crusted golden brown.

Sunday Supper
Rosemary Chicken Supreme

Serves 4

This dish is an 'old school' classic, for sure. I think every culture, every family cook, has their own version of chicken supreme, which simply refers to a boneless chicken breast in sauce, or in my case, a succulent chicken breast soaked in buttery white sauce.

Irish farmhouse cooks have been preparing these dishes for generations, and I am confident my great grandmother would have served her chicken supreme when she worked as a cook in Boston, pairing it with seasonal vegetables from their garden.

My family has always loved to make simple and delicious white sauce chicken dishes, as they speak so much of comfort and of a sense of home. Over the years, I have added bright flavors to my version — fresh rosemary, white wine, artichokes, and garlic — making this chicken supreme my very own, a version I am happy to share with you.

CHICKEN SUPREME INGREDIENTS

1 tablespoon vegetable oil
1 tablespoon of butter
4 chicken breast fillets (2 pounds)
12 ounces artichokes hearts (cut in quarters)
Fine sea salt and pepper

SAUCE INGREDIENTS

4 tablespoons butter
1 medium (3 tablespoons) shallot finely chopped
2 garlic cloves (minced)
¾ cup heavy whipping cream
¾ cup chicken stock
¼ cup dry white wine
½ cup Dubliner Irish cheese (finely grated)
1 tablespoon rosemary (finely chopped)

HOW TO MAKE

1. Season the chicken fillets with freshly ground pepper and sea salt.

2. In a large skillet, melt the butter and oil over medium high heat. Add the chicken breasts and sear on both sides until they are browned. Remove the chicken from the skillet for a few minutes to make the sauce.

3. Preheat the oven to 400°F.

4. To make the sauce, melt the butter in the same skillet the chicken fillets were browned. Add the shallot and cook until for a few minutes, until it is soft and translucent. Add the garlic and rosemary and cook for one minute until fragrant, being careful not to burn the garlic. Add the wine and cook on medium for about 5 minutes or until the wine has almost evaporated. Add the chicken stock and cream and cook for a few minutes. Stir in the Dubliner Irish cheese until the cheese has melted.

5. Add the chicken fillets back into the skillet and spoon the sauce on top. Arrange the artichokes hearts all around the chicken. Bake the chicken supreme in the oven for a further 18–20 minutes until the chicken is fully cooked and firm to the touch (internal temperature of 165°F).

6. To serve, place a chicken breast in the center of each plate and spoon more sauce on top.

Crumbled Corn Beef
& Sweet Potato Tart

❧ Serves 6 ❧

High Tea in Ireland includes a hot, light savory dish, followed by bread and tea. It is a tradition that Irish immigrants brought along with them to America during the Gilded Age, and I can imagine the pomp and ceremony of young Irish immigrants, such as my great grandmother, serving tea to wealthy ladies in grand houses in Boston.

Despite its ubiquity as a staple Irish food, my husband and I did not eat corn beef until we moved to America. It is a food more Irish American, relatively unknown in Ireland. The corned beef from the English Market in Cork is seen as something of a rarity. Still, my sons are proudly Irish American themselves, and we certainly enjoy a corn beef and cabbage meal on St. Patrick's Day.

What do we do with any leftover corned beef after our Irish feasts? I typically use it to prepare wonderful sweet potato and corned beef tarts, sometimes referred to as a "quiche." As my grandmother taught me, nothing should ever be wasted! And I like to believe that she would have happily found a home for these tarts on one of her lady's tea trays.

PASTRY INGREDIENTS

1¼ cups all-purpose flour (sifted)
¼ teaspoon salt
7 tablespoons unsalted butter (chilled)
2–4 tablespoons ice cold water

FILLING INGREDIENTS

7 ounces Corn Beef (crumbled into small pieces)
2 tablespoons olive oil
2 medium leeks (white parts and some green)
4 large eggs (beaten)
1 cup whipping cream
1 sweet potato (cooked and mashed)
¼ teaspoon fine sea salt
⅛ teaspoon white pepper
1 cup of sharp cheddar cheese
½ cup Parmesan cheese

HOW TO MAKE

1. To make the pastry, combine flour and salt in a medium size bowl or food processor. Use a pastry fork or processor to cut in the butter until it resembles coarse crumbs. Add the cold water 1 tablespoon at a time and mix until the dough is moist enough to hold together to form a ball. Flatten into a disc and wrap and refrigerate for at least 30 minutes.

2. On a lightly floured surface roll out dough into a circle about 11-inches in diameter for a 9-inch pie plate or fluted tart pan. Trim off any excess pastry and prick the bottom of the dough with a fork.

3. Preheat oven to 375°F. To blind bake the pastry, line with a double layer of foil and bake for 10 minutes to prevent browning. Remove foil and bake pastry for a few more minutes until golden brown. Remove from oven and cool on a wire rack and leave oven on.

4. To make filling, in a large skillet add 2 tablespoons of olive oil and sauté the leeks for 3–4 minutes or until soft and fragrant and remove from heat.

5. In a food processor or mixing bowl combine eggs, cream, mashed sweet potato, salt and pepper.

6. To assemble the quiche, layer the corn beef and leek and the cheeses and then pour the egg mixture on top.

7. Bake for 30–35 minutes or until the egg sets and is firm to the touch.

8. Allow the quiche to sit for at least 15 minutes before serving.

Warm Apple Dumplings

Warm crumbly pastry with a sweet apple filling is the ultimate comfort food for any family gathering, with apple dumpling roots going back to the 17th century in the Celtic lands. The word dumpling refers to a dough base that is steamed, boiled and it can also mean baked.

Encasing a whole baked apple and baking it in dough is one of the purest forms of tasting the flavors of the fruit, without nothing but crumbly pastry to compete with its natural goodness. Try serving it with vanilla ice cream, and you will be in heaven!

PASTRY INGREDIENTS

2¼ cups of all-purpose flour
¼ teaspoon of salt
⅔ cup of shortening
6–8 tablespoons of ice water

EGG WASH INGREDIENTS

1 egg (beaten with a little water)

APPLE FILLING INGREDIENTS

6 medium size baking apples
3–4 tablespoons of brown sugar
2 tablespoons of butter

SAUCE INGREDIENTS

1 cup water
¾ cup sugar
¼ teaspoon cinnamon
¼ teaspoon nutmeg
1½ tablespoons butter
1 drop of red food coloring

HOW TO MAKE

1. Preheat the oven to 400°F.

2. To make the pastry, combine the flour and salt in a large bowl and rub in the shortening until the mixture resembles breadcrumbs. Using a knife, stir in the ice water until a dough is formed adding a little extra water if necessary. Form the dough in a rectangular shape disc with hands and then cut that in to 6 equal pieces to make it easier to roll out into square shapes.

3. Core and peel the apples and place each one in the center of prepared pastry. Spoon a little butter and brown sugar inside the center of each apple. Brush the inside edges of the pastry with a little water and pull up to the center to completely cover the apple like a little package. Brush the outside of the dumpling with egg wash.

4. Grease a medium size baking dish and set the dumplings gently in to the pan. Place the dumplings in the oven and bake them for 45 minutes until the pastry is golden brown and the apples are soft.

5. While the apples are baking, prepare the sauce by boiling together the water, sugar, spices, and a little food coloring and then whisking in the butter.

6. To serve, place the apple dumpling in the center of a dish and pour of the sauce. Best enjoyed with a spoonful of vanilla ice-cream.

White Chocolate Buttermilk Waffle Berry Pudding

❧ *Serves 6–8* ❦

Irish people adore bread. We have many unique types, such as soda bread, brown wheaten bread, batch loaves, Waterford Blaas and Belfast baps. As immigrants, we turn to baking bread to keep in touch with our cultural traditions. Bread helps recreate the comforts of home, especially during times of transition.

Irish immigrants like my great grandparents were also often very frugal folks, hating to see anything go to waste. Comforting, eggy bread pudding is an ideal way to use up day-old bread in a delicious way. I can close my eyes and still see the old AGA stove of my childhood, bread pudding baking inside with golden raisins, brown sugar, and nutmeg, the wonderful aromas filling the farmhouse kitchen.

I have added white chocolate, raspberries, and using fluffy buttermilk waffles to this decadent version, and I hope you enjoy!

PUDDING INGREDIENTS

1 tablespoon butter
12 ounces buttermilk waffles
2 cups mixed berries (raspberries and blueberries)
8 ounces (1 cup) white chocolate chips

CUSTARD SAUCE INGREDIENTS

16 fluid ounces (2 cups) crème fraiche or sour cream
¼ cup heavy cream
¼ cup fine granulated sugar
2 teaspoons vanilla
4 large eggs (beaten)
1 tablespoon cornstarch
1 teaspoon lemon zest

WHITE CHOCOLATE SAUCE

½ cup of heavy cream
1 cup white chocolate chunks

GARNISH

¼ cup freeze dried berries (chopped)

HOW TO MAKE

1. Grease a 9 x 13-inch pan with 1 tablespoon of room temperature butter.

2. Cut the waffles into small pieces and arrange on the bottom of prepared pan. Spoon over half of the berries and chocolate on top, and then repeat the layers by adding the remaining waffles, berries, and chocolate. Whisk the eggs, sour cream, cream, sugar, vanilla, cornstarch, lemon zest and sugar. Pour mixture over the waffles and then pat the pudding with a fork and shake the pan to distribute evenly.

3. Allow at least 1 hour for the waffles to soak and absorb the custard (or even better cover and leave overnight to soak).

4. Preheat the oven to 350°F.

5. Bake the pudding for 30 minutes. The pudding will be cooked when the outside is crunchy, and the inside is firm but soft.

6. To make the white chocolate sauce, heat the cream in a small saucepan and bring it up to boiling temperature. Remove cream from the heat and pour it over the white chocolate chips, stirring until they have melted.

7. To garnish, sprinkle a small handful of crumbled freeze-dried raspberries. Serve the pudding warm with the white chocolate sauce on the side.

Chapter Three

The Greening Shore

Celebrating all that is Irish on America's greening shore

The story of the Irish in America is of a resilient people who made it despite the odds, and markers of their culinary traditions and Irish heritage can still be seen today melding with contemporary American cuisine to become staples of this country's food culture.

Consider, for example, Edmund McIlhenny, founder of the McIlhenny Company, maker of Tabasco Red Pepper Sauce, whose ancestors came from Donegal. Consider, too, Bananas Foster, one of my favorite desserts, created in New Orleans by an Irish family called Brennan.

There's evidence in so much of American cuisine of the influence of those brave Irish immigrants who crossed the sea.

The Lady's Maid and the Carpenter

The waning months of 1899 found young Etta McGarvey at work in the home of her adopted family in Plymouth, Massachusetts.

She likely polished the Woods' silver, set the tables, took meticulous care of her lady's fine things. I can see her taking walks by the harbor in those first few years in America, gazing out across the wide Atlantic, dreaming of her parents and sisters back in Donegal, of the mountains and cool breezes, of the smells, the wide-open green landscapes of her home. At the time, there were few other Irish people in such a quintessentially English part of America's northeast, and perhaps Etta felt lonely, rarely having an opportunity to speak familiar words that those around her would understand or appreciate.

It was during those heady days that the Woods family often employed skilled men to work on their home. One such man was a young John McNeill, recent immigrant from County Down. John travelled on the train from Brookline to Plymouth, carrying

his own bag of tools and a reputation for good, clean carpentry work.

I can picture my great-grandfather, walking to the Woods' residence from the train station, ringing that grand doorbell, cap in hand, only to find Etta on the other side. Perhaps their eyes met as John handed Etta his letter of recommendation. Perhaps my great-grandmother smiled when she heard that warm, familiar Irish accent. Could they both feel then that fate had taken its turn?

The Woods family arranged lodging for John in town as he worked on their home. Over the days and weeks that followed, Etta had several opportunities to steal outside, and I can almost feel, even now, the familiar anticipation of a young girl with a crush, eager and hoping for a chance to talk to the newly arrived Irishman. Even though morals of the time dictated those single young men and woman refrain from social contact, Etta and John likely began walking and talking together, passing the time as the leaves turned red, New England slipping quietly from spring into fall.

I let my imagination continue telling me my great grandparents' love story. How Etta would secretly meet John by the harbor wall in the evening, where they would talk of home, of their experiences since they had arrived in America, of their dreams for the future—Etta's heart light as a feather when she was with John; John was carried away by the elegant young woman from Donegal that had swept into his life so suddenly.

Eventually, my great grandfather would complete his job at the Woods house. As he prepared to return to Brookline, he exchanged addresses with Etta, and in the weeks and months that followed, eager letters passed back and forth between them.

John worked every moment he had, saved every dollar he earned, likely looking forward to the day when he could formally bring Etta back to Boston as his fiancé. Back to the city's greening shore, where the Irish had made a real home, a community, in America. Where they might make a life, a mark, of their own.

The Irish Way

For many years, I too, have strived to make my own mark on the Irish American cultural landscape.

Since first coming to the United States, I have crafted menus and taught Irish cooking classes extolling the beautiful simplicity of Celtic cuisine. Using fresh ingredients such as grass-fed Irish butter or wild salmon and Irish oats, my intention has always been to carry the torch my ancestors lit, proudly declaring Irish food as a cuisine worthy of celebration.

I invite you now to come celebrate all that is Irish with me with some of my most requested recipes, dishes that will make any St. Patrick's celebration come to life.

CHAPTER THREE
Irish Celebration Foods

Kilkeel Crab & Apple in Cucumber Cups
(page 72)

Celtic Sea Smoked Mackerel with Crispy Garlic Toasts

One of the benefits of going home after living abroad for a while is the wonderful, warm hospitality that my family and friends spoil me with. It is always so great to celebrate with loved ones after periods of absence, and this recipe is one of my favorite appetizers from family gatherings in Ireland. Perfected by my Aunt Sally, these superb toasts are often served as welcome nibbles before a family dinner.

Smoked mackerel has tons of flavor and is hard to beat when complemented with hot, peppery horseradish, slightly sour crème fraiche, and a citrus lemon tang.

Mackerel is a striking tiger-striped fish and is also packed with healthy omega-3 oils. It is abundant in the seas of Ireland, and also makes for an incredible pâté. Enjoy!

MACKEREL PÂTÉ INGREDIENTS

8 ounces of smoked mackerel (skins removed and flaked)
7 ounces of crème fraiche
1 teaspoon Dijon mustard
1 tablespoon horseradish sauce
1 tablespoon lemon juice
1 teaspoon of zest
2 tablespoons chives (finely chopped)
Freshly ground black pepper

TOAST INGREDIENTS

6 slices of rustic sourdough bread
1 garlic clove (cut in half)
2 tablespoons olive oil
Coarse sea salt

HOW TO MAKE

1. To make the pâté, remove the brown piece in the center of the mackerel and all the skin. Check there are no bones and remove them.

2. In a food processor, combine the mackerel, crème fraiche, Dijon mustard, horseradish, lemon juice and zest, and pepper and blend for about a minute. Pulse for a few more seconds until the crème fraiche has absorbed into the mackerel.

3. Spoon the pâté into a bowl and garnish with finely chopped chives.

4. To make the garlic toasts, preheat the oven to 425°F. Rub the cut garlic over the bread and then using a pastry brush coat a little olive oil over the bread. Place the bread on a baking sheet and bake for 8–10 minutes turning around halfway. The toasts should be crispy and browned when ready. Serve immediately sprinkled with a little bit of sea salt.

5. Place the toasts around the mackerel pâté bowl and enjoy!

Kilkeel Crab & Apple in Cucumber Cups

Serves 4

Kilkeel is one of the main fishing ports on the County Down coast, close to where my grandparents ran their bed and breakfast. The fisheries there, with their brightly colored boats, are known for producing delicious, sustainably sourced brown crab. They supply this delicious crustacean to high-end restaurants in Ireland and around the world.

Brown crab is known for its soft, sweet, delicate taste, and is incredibly high in protein and vitamin B12. The brown crab contains two types of meat—white meat from the claws and legs, and the more strongly flavored brown meat of the body of the crab.

I tend to use the white crab meat for this recipe, which has a milder, flakier texture than brown meat. For a stunning presentation at a more elegant occasion, try this dish with a garnish of caviar. It's just the right size for a party appetizer, or as a lovely starter at a family celebration.

CUCUMBER CUPS INGREDIENTS

1 English cucumber (scraped and cut in to 8)
4 ounces fresh cooked crab meat (white meat from claws and legs)
1 ounce Granny Smith apple (grated)
2 tablespoons lime juice
1 teaspoon lime zest
2 tablespoons crème fraiche
2 tablespoons mayonnaise
1 tablespoon shallots (finely chopped)
1 tablespoon flat leafed parsley (chopped) plus 8 sprigs for garnish
Dash of McIlhenny Tabasco sauce
Fine sea salt and freshly ground black pepper

GARNISH

8 small red chili (very finely chopped)

HOW TO MAKE

1. To prepare the cucumbers, scrape most of the green skin with a vegetable peeler leaving some for color and texture. Using a sharp knife, cut the cucumber in 1-inch length pieces. Use a small melon ball scoop to cut out center of each to create a cup.

2. If using fresh crab meat pick the crab and remove any shells.

3. Finely dice the shallot and flat leaf parsley.

4. Grate the apple finely and squeeze the lime juice over the top of it.

5. Combine the apple mixture, lime zest, crab meat, shallots, tobacco sauce and chopped parsley.

6. Finally, add the crème fraiche and mayonnaise and taste to adjust the seasoning with fine sea salt and pepper. Adjust the consistency by adding some more crème fraiche and mayonnaise.

7. To serve, fill each cup with the crab and apple salad. Garnish with a flat parsley leaf and sprinkle a little of the finely diced red chili.

Asparagus Salad with Sweet Peppers & Baby Arugula

The R.M.S Titanic was built in Belfast, Ireland and its fatal story on April 14, 1912, has a special place in my heart. My grandfather waved goodbye to the Titanic on his father's shoulders on its maiden voyage to Southampton, England and my grandparents felt very emotional about its sinking, passing on an intrigue about all things Titanic.

Over the years I have hosted a few Titanic inspired dinner parties in my home, and this is my version adapted from the cookbook *The Last Night on the Titanic*, drawn from the original menu.

Believe it or not, this fine salad was part of the extravagant first-class marathon menu of eleven courses.

SALAD INGREDIENTS

1½ pounds spring asparagus (snap off woody ends)
½ sweet yellow pepper (quartered/seeds and membranes removed)
½ sweet red pepper (quartered/seeds and membranes removed)
4 cups arugula (also known as Rocket)
1½ ounces Parmesan Reggiano (thinly shaved)
Salt and freshly ground black pepper
Olive oil

VINAIGRETTE INGREDIENTS

3 tablespoons champagne vinegar
1½ tablespoons of shallots (minced)
1 teaspoon Dijon mustard
1 teaspoon raw honey
¼ teaspoon saffron threads
1 teaspoon boiling water
6 tablespoons extra-virgin olive oil

HOW TO MAKE

1. Preheat oven to 425°F. Spread asparagus and peppers in a single layer on roasting pan and drizzle with olive oil. Season with salt and freshly ground black pepper. Roast for 7–8 minutes until crisp tender.

2. Preheat oven to 450°F. Spread the bell peppers in a single layer on a roasting pan and drizzle with olive oil. Roast until tender and charred for 18–20 minutes. Cool and chop.

3. To make the salad dressing, soften the saffron by adding boiling water and let it stand for a few minutes to soften. Whisk in the champagne vinegar, minced shallots, honey, and mustard then finally add the olive oil in a slow steady drizzle. Season with salt and pepper to taste.

4. In a large bowl, combine the arugula with enough vinaigrette to coat the greens.

5. To assemble the salad, arrange the arugula in the center of each plate. Arrange the asparagus spears and the roasted peppers. Finish by drizzling a little more vinaigrette over the salad and sprinkle with the fresh Parmesan Reggiano shavings.

Irish Stout & Onion Soup with Blue Cheese

❧ *Serves 4–6* ☙

This is my Irish spin on the classic French Onion Soup with the subtle hint of hoppy Irish stout added to the broth. The "blissful" layers of flavor in this soup are complex and rich with the caramelized onions, stout infused beef stock, and the tangy blue cheese.

Cashel Blue is one of Ireland's best-known blue cheeses, but it is worth searching out Kearney Blue from County Down if you venture north. Made by Paul McClean to resemble the dry-stone walls of his townland, it won Best Irish at Nantwich Cheese Show with its second make.

This soup is a wonderful comfort food for a cold day by the fireside but can also be a fun dish when served outdoors complimented by your favorite stout or hoppy beer.

SOUP INGREDIENTS

2 tablespoons olive oil
3 large (1½ pounds) sweet Vidalia onions (thinly sliced)
5 cloves of garlic (peeled and chopped)
2 sprig of thyme (leaves removed from the stems)
1 tablespoon all-purpose flour (dissolved in a little water)
2 tablespoons brown sugar
6 cups beef stock
1½ cups Irish stout
2 tablespoons Worcestershire sauce
¼ teaspoon kosher salt
¼ teaspoon freshly ground black pepper

BLUE CHEESE CROUTONS

6 slices of baguette
1 clove garlic clove (peeled and cut in half)
2 tablespoons butter
½ cup (2 ounces) blue cheese

HOW TO MAKE

1. Heat the oil and butter in a large stock pot over medium high heat. Add the onions, garlic and the brown sugar stirring constantly. Reduce heat to medium/low and cook the onions and garlic slowly for 20 minutes or until they are light brown in color.

2. Add the thyme, flour, beer, Worcestershire sauce, salt, pepper, and beef stock to the onions and garlic.

3. Bring the soup to a boil and then lower the temperature to simmering point for about 20 more minutes until the onions are very soft. Taste soup and adjust seasoning.

4. To make the croutons, preheat oven to 400°F. Slice the bread and rub with the cut garlic. Brush both sides with melted butter and place on a baking sheet. Bake in the oven for just a few minutes until the bread is a golden color but still soft inside.

5. Preheat the soup bowls in the oven to prep for serving.

6. Just before serving the soup, top one side of the bread with Cashel blue cheese and broil until the cheese is bubbly and brown.

7. To serve, fill preheated bowls with the soup then place a slice of the melted blue cheese toast on top of each bowl.

Dublin Lawyer Lobster

Serves 4

Lobsters are caught all around the Irish coast and are widely available from most fish markets on the island. Even though it is quite plentiful in Ireland, lobster is still considered one of the most decadent meats of choice, worthy of special occasions which is probably why I had never tasted lobster until my husband, and I drove to Maine one weekend to taste their famous cold-water lobster. It made me a believer for life!

Legend has it that the quirky name given to this Irish dish was chosen because, just like the sauce, lawyers are rich, and they are known to enjoy a 'wee dram' of Irish whiskey to wash down their expensive lunches after a day at the Dublin courthouses.

We hope you will consider this wonderful Irish twist on lobster for your next celebration dinner. Thankfully, you do not need to be a rich Dublin lawyer to try it!

LOBSTER INGREDIENTS

4 cold water lobster tails (7 ounces) fresh or thawed from frozen
4 slices of rustic sour dough bread

GARLIC BUTTER INGREDIENTS

4 tablespoons unsalted butter
1 clove of garlic
¼ teaspoon salt
Freshly ground black pepper, to taste

WHISKEY CREAM INGREDIENTS

1 tablespoon butter
1 clove of garlic
4 tablespoons Irish whiskey
5 tablespoons heavy cream
1 tablespoon fresh lemon juice
2 tablespoons chives (finely chopped)

HOW TO MAKE

1. Preheat grill to medium high heat.

2. To prepare the lobster for grilling, use kitchen scissors to cut through the back of the lobster tails lengthwise, stopping when the tail fin has been reached. Using a knife cut the lobster tails down the line cut with scissors to expose the lobster for the meat to cook evenly.

3. Brush the lobster generously with the garlic butter. Place the lobster meat side down first and grill for around 4–5 minutes. Brush with more lemon garlic butter and turn them over to cook for another 4 minutes. The flesh will be white and pink and firm to the touch when ready.

4. Brush the sourdough bread with the garlic butter and place on the grill to toast and lightly char.

5. To make the Dublin Lawyer sauce, heat the butter until foaming in a skillet over medium high heat and add the garlic. Add the whiskey to the pan (tilting it towards the flame to ignite). Once the flames have died, add the cream and allow it to reduce for a few minutes cooking until the sauce begins to slightly thicken. Add the freshly squeezed lemon juice and stir.

6. To serve, place the lobster tail in a bowl, pour the sauce over the cooked lobster tails and serve with a piece of sourdough toast for sopping.

Aged Gaelic Steaks with an Irish Whiskey Cream Sauce

Serves 4

Irish beef, farmed in Ireland for thousands of years, is known for its unique flavor and high quality thanks to the grass-fed grazing of the cattle, and the smaller scale of Irish farms with their lush green fields. Prime aged beef of a similar quality is the star of this otherwise simple, straightforward dish.

Peter Hannan from Moira ages his in a Himalayan Salt-Chamber. Salt-aging is also done by Joe Quail in Banbridge. Pat Whelan in Tipperary and Hugh Maguire from Co. Meath are other butchers of great renown.

Ideally, if you can, purchase your beef from a butcher who has aged his meat from ten to fourteen days it will make a big difference in terms of the flavor of the recipe, which is worthy of a milestone birthday party, graduation, or other special occasion. Higher-end, choice cuts of beef such as a porterhouse or New York strip are considered celebratory meats, and it is best to choose well when at the butcher's shop, as the cut of beef will determine its eventual tenderness and quality.

Irish whiskey pairs well with steak dishes like this one because of its wonderful, complex flavor which is not diminished in the deglazing process. Whiskey and steak, the perfect Irish couple!

STEAK INGREDIENTS

4 New York steaks or 2 porterhouse cut steaks (aged and cut 1-inch thick)
Sea salt
Freshly ground black pepper
1 tablespoon of butter
1 tablespoon of vegetable oil

SAUCE INGREDIENTS

1 tablespoon of salted butter
1 shallot (finely chopped)
¼ cup of Irish whiskey
¼ cup chicken stock
¾ cup of heavy whipping cream
1 tablespoon fresh parsley (finely chopped)

HOW TO MAKE

1. Melt 1 tablespoon of the butter and oil on medium high heat in a large skillet and season the room temperature steaks liberally with freshly ground black pepper and sea salt. When the butter is foaming, add the steaks one at a time to the pan and turn them after 20–30 seconds to sear both sides (do not overcrowd to get a nice sear if not using a large size skillet). Lower the heat to medium heat (3–4 minutes for rare, 4–5 minutes for medium rare, 4–5 minutes for medium, 5–6 minutes for well done) turning each steak halfway.

2. Wrap the steaks in aluminum foil and transfer the steaks to a low temperature oven or covered in a warming drawer.

3. To make the Irish whiskey sauces, add the butter to the pan with the shallots and cook for about a minute scraping the flavorful brown bits. Deglaze the pan adding the Irish whiskey and chicken stock and reduce slightly on a low simmer. Add the cream to the pan cooking to reduce and gently simmer until the cream begins to thicken.

4. Season with salt and pepper and stir in the fresh chopped parsley.

5. To serve, pour the sauce over the pan seared steaks.

Pan-Roasted Fillet of Halibut with a Lemon & Herb Butter Sauce

Serves 4

This lean white fish from the Atlantic Ocean pairs beautifully with the depth and richness of the sauce which compliments well with the sweetness of the fish.

Wherever you are in Ireland, because of the proximity to our shores, it allows us to enjoy the bounty of the sea with optimum freshness. Halibut is widely available in Ireland as an Atlantic fish but can also be easily sourced here in North America. Enjoy those flaky chunks of fish as they soak up the sauce!

FISH INGREDIENTS

4 halibut fillets (4–6 ounces) pin bones removed and trimmed with the skin on
1–2 tablespoons olive oil
Sea salt and freshly ground black pepper
2 sprigs of thyme

GARLIC & HERB BUTTER SAUCE

2 ounces butter
1 clove of garlic (crushed)
1 tablespoon mixed herbs (parsley, tarragon, and chives) finely chopped
2 tablespoons lemon juice
Zest of one lemon

PICKLED RED ONIONS INGREDIENTS

1 small red onion (finely sliced)
½ teaspoon sugar
½ teaspoon salt
¾ cup of apple cider vinegar

GARNISH

Small bunch of watercress

HOW TO MAKE

1. To make the pickled red onions for the garnish, add the vinegar, salt, and sugar to 2 cups of water and boil gently for 2 minutes. Remove from the heat and set aside.

2. To prepare the halibut, use a sharp knife to score the skin and season the fillets with salt and freshly ground black pepper.

3. Heat the oil in a skillet over medium high heat and add the thyme sprig. Once the oil starts to sizzle, place the halibut fillets skin downside down and reduce the heat to medium.

4. Cook the fillets for 4 minutes and then turn and cook for about 3 minutes more (the fish is ready when the thickest part of the halibut is flakey and opaque). Remove the fish from the pan and place in a warm oven. Discard the thyme.

5. To make the lemon and herb garlic butter sauce, melt the butter in a small clean saucepan and add the garlic cooking for just under a minute (being careful not to burn the garlic). Remove from the heat and slowly whisk in the lemon juice. Stir in the chopped herbs at the end. To serve, place the halibut skin side up on the plate and spoon a little lemon and herb garlic sauce over the top. Strain the red onions for the garnish and combine with the watercress, toss in a little olive oil, and sprinkle a little on each fillet of halibut.

Padraig's Roasted Potato Cups

Serves 4

No Irish celebration would be complete without at least one potato dish, and these beauties are a perfect way to feed your party guests upon arrival. The added flavor of earthy Portobello mushrooms paired with aged Irish cheddar cheese and drizzled with truffle-infused oil are truly divine.

Make these scrumptious one-bite cups for Irish Feast days or as cocktail party nibbles. You can also get creative and try other filling combinations. Some of my favorites are bacon and blue cheese, or tomato, cheddar, and basil.

POTATO CUPS INGREDIENTS

1¼ pound baby potatoes (red and gold varieties)
2 tablespoons olive oil
Kosher salt and pepper

MUSHROOM FILLING INGREDIENTS

1½ tablespoons olive oil
5 tablespoons shallots (finely chopped)
8 ounces portobello mushrooms (finely chopped)
2 cloves of garlic (finely chopped)
1½ ounces aged Irish cheddar cheese (1 tablespoon grated/the remaining shaved)
Salt and pepper to season

GARNISH FINISHING INGREDIENTS

1 tablespoon truffle oil (to drizzle)
Chives (cut in to ½-inch pieces for a garnish)

HOW TO MAKE

1. Preheat the oven to 400°F.

2. Cut each potato in half. Using a melon baller, scoop out a hole in the center in the cut side of each potato half. Use a knife to slice a small piece of the skin side of each potato so they will stand straight when plating and serving.

3. Brush potatoes with olive oil and sprinkle with salt and pepper. Bake on a roasting pan, cut side down, for 15 minutes or until the potatoes are soft when pierced with a fork.

4. To make the mushroom filling, sauté the finely chopped mushrooms and shallots in olive oil until the mushrooms are a deep brown and the shallots have caramelized. Stir in the garlic and cook for 1 minute. Remove from the heat and stir in 1 tablespoon of finely grated aged cheddar. Season with salt and pepper.

5. Use a small teaspoon to fill each warm potato cup. Before serving drizzle a little truffle oil and top each potato with a piece of chive and shaving of aged Irish cheddar cheese.

Dublin Born Beef Wellington

⤳ *Serves 4–6* ⤲

The association with the Duke of Wellington, may not be celebrated by the Irish, but it nevertheless it does have a surprising Irish connection. The Duke of Wellington was born in Dublin Ireland in 1769, into the home of an upper-class Anglo-Irish family as Arthur Wellesley and rose to great fame from his Dublin roots.

The dish is said to be created in celebration of the Duke of Wellington's victory over Napoléon at the Battle of Waterloo. Wonderful, show stopping party dish named in honor of our Dublin born hero!

BEEF INGREDIENTS

3 pounds of center cut beef tenderloin (trimmed)
2 tablespoons butter
2 tablespoons Dijon mustard
10 slices of prosciutto/Parma ham
1 pound of puff pastry (thawed to room temperature)
1 large egg (beaten with a little water)
Coarse sea salt

MUSHROOM FILLING INGREDIENTS

1½ pounds of mushrooms (white button or a mixed variety)
2 tablespoons of shallots (diced)
3 cloves of garlic (diced)
3 sprigs thyme (stems removed/2 teaspoons leaves)
3 tablespoons olive oil
Kosher salt and pepper

HOW TO MAKE

1. Tuck the thinner end of the tenderloin in and secure it with kitchen twine to create an even log shape, using more twine, as necessary.

2. Season the tenderloin generously with kosher salt and ground black pepper. Add the butter into a hot heavy based skillet and sear the tenderloin for just a minute on all sides. Set aside to cool.

3. To make the mushroom filling, pulse the mushrooms, shallots, garlic, thyme, salt, and pepper together in the food processor until they are finely chopped. Add olive oil to the skillet and cook over medium high heat until most of the liquid has evaporated (that will take 6–7 minutes).

4. Layer the prosciutto out flat, overlapping over a sheet of plastic wrap to form a rectangle large enough to cover the beef. Spread the mushroom filling evenly over the prosciutto.

5. Remove any twine from the beef and brush it all over with Dijon mustard. Slowly roll the beef up tightly in the prepared prosciutto to keep its shape and make an even size log. Seal the sides, and chill in the refrigerator for at least 30 minutes.

6. Preheat the oven to 425°F and line a rimmed baking sheet with parchment paper.

7. Roll out the puff pastry on a lightly floured surface, wide enough to wrap the beef. Take the beef from the refrigerator, removing the plastic wrap. Place the beef in the center of the prepared puff pastry, and fold over the edges, sealing with the egg wash using a pastry brush. Trim any excess pastry and brush the outside with the egg wash. Season with coarse salt.

8. Bake in the oven for 25–30 minutes medium rare (the ends of the beef will be less pink than the center). Allow to rest for 10 minutes before slicing.

Connemara Mountain Lamb with Mixed Carrot & Rosemary Jus

Serves 4

Connemara in the west of Ireland, is known for its rolling valleys, high mountains, lakes, and the numerous sheep that roam the hillsides. My father, a sheep farmer from County Armagh, would buy spring lambs from Connemara each year and transport them up to our farm where they would feast on the lush green pastures of mid-Ulster, growing pleasantly plump in the process—always a good thing for farmers!

Irish lamb is rich and flavorful, but not too gamey, and no trip to Ireland would be complete without tasting it at least once. It is a true Irish feast food.

In May 2014, I had the honor of cooking a celebratory Irish meal with Chefs Noel McMeel and Stephen Holland from the Lough Erne Resort, and with well-known cookbook author, Margaret Johnston, at the James Beard House in New York. Our menu was entitled *The Three Shades of Green*, and this is the lamb entrée that we served. I hope you enjoy it making this recipe as much as we enjoyed crafting it.

LAMB SHANK INGREDIENTS

3 tablespoons olive oil
4 lamb shanks (¾–1 pound each)
1 large carrot (diced)
1 onion (diced)
3 cups beef stock (and enough water to cover shanks)
1 bay leaf
2 cloves of garlic (diced)
4 sprigs of thyme
4 sprigs of rosemary (for garnish)
Kosher salt and fresh ground pepper

ROASTED CARROT INGREDIENTS

3 carrots (purple and yellow tri color variety lightly peeled)
12 baby carrots
2 tablespoons of butter
1 teaspoon of balsamic vinegar
Kosher salt and pepper

ROSEMARY JUS INGREDIENTS

½ onion (diced)
1 garlic clove (crushed)
½ cup red wine
1 cup veal stock (or chicken stock)
¼ cup beef stock
2 teaspoons sugar
Sprigs of rosemary

HOW TO MAKE

1. Season the lamb shanks with kosher salt and freshly ground black pepper. In a large skillet, heat the olive oil over medium heat. Cook the lamb on all sides until browned, about 5 minutes.

2. Transfer the lamb shanks on to a large deep oven proof dish. Add the onion, carrot, garlic, bay leaf and thyme to the dish.

3. Add the beef stock and enough water to cover the lamb shanks until submerged in the stock. Cover with Cling Film (Glad Wrap) and Parchment Foil.

4. Preheat the oven to 350°F and cook for 3–4 hours until the meat is tender and falls off at the bone.

5. To make the roasted vegetables, prepare the carrots ahead by cutting them in half and cook in seasoned water for 10 minutes and then refresh in an ice-cold water bath. Cut the carrots in half and set aside until ready to roast. Transfer to a baking pan and drizzle with melted butter and a dash of balsamic vinegar and roast for 10 minutes or until they are beginning to caramelize.

6. Using a slotted spoon, transfer the lamb shanks to a warming drawer or plate and cover to keep warm. Strain the cooking liquid from the lamb through a fine sieve into a clean saucepan, pressing the vegetables through with the back of a spoon. Cook over low heat and reduce.

7. To make the rosemary jus, sear off the onion and garlic in a large sauté pan with olive oil until golden brown. Add the red wine and reduce by two thirds. Add the veal stock, beef stock, rosemary, sugar, salt, and pepper and reduce heat. Once the correct consistency is achieved add the reduced cooking liquor to finish and roasted carrots.

8. To serve, place a spoon of the colcannon in the center of each warmed plate. Set the lamb shank on the side and then spoon the roasted vegetables and jus all over the shank. Garnish with a sprig of rosemary.

Nana's Lemon Meringue Tart

⤳ Serves 6 ⤲

A crowd-pleasing dessert to enjoy any time of the year, featuring tangy lemon curd, a buttery crust and melt in your mouth puffy meringue!

Lemon Meringue is in the forefront of my memory when I think of my grandmother, who I affectionately called "Nana." I can remember the love that graced this dessert when it was presented at her dinner table as I visited when growing up. A firm family favorite.

I suggest that you serve it with lashings of whipped cream just the way I remember it at my Nana's house in County Armagh.

CRUST INGREDIENTS

Baked pie dough (see recipe for Bakewell Tart for crust)

LEMON CURD FILLING INGREDIENTS

12 fluid ounces (1½ cups) water
6 ounces (¾ cup) fine granulated sugar
4 tablespoons cornstarch
¾ cup of lemon juice
2 ounces butter (room temperature)
5 egg yolks (beaten)
Zest of 3 lemons

MERINGUE INGREDIENTS

3 egg whites
6 ounces (¾ cup) fine granulated sugar
¼ teaspoon cream of tartar

HOW TO MAKE

1. To make the lemon curd, measure the water and then use a few tablespoons to blend the cornstarch and set aside. In a medium saucepan add the water, lemon zest, lemon juice and sugar in a medium size saucepan. Whisk in the blended cornstarch and water, and then stir for a few minutes until the mixture begins to thicken.

2. Remove the lemon mixture from the heat and whisk in the butter, a little bit at a time.

3. Wait a few minutes to let the lemon mixture cool, and then slowly whisk in the beaten egg yolks. When the eggs are fully incorporated, return the lemon curd to a low heat, stirring constantly until it thickens to a pudding like consistency (thick enough to coat the back of a spoon, or the curd will not set correctly).

4. Pour the curd directly on to the crust, and cover with plastic wrap pressed directly on the curd and place in the refrigerator for at least an hour to cool completely.

5. To make the meringue, preheat the oven to 350°F. Whisk the egg whites and cream of tartar in a large bowl until stiff peaks appear. Slowly add the sugar 1 teaspoon at a time until the meringue is very stiff (you should be able to turn the bowl upside down and the meringue will stay in place).

6. The meringue can be piped on using a bag or spooned on directly to the lemon curd.

7. Bake the pie in the lowest rack in the oven for 20–25 minutes until the meringue sets.

8. Allow the baked lemon meringue to rest at room temperature for an hour, and then for another 4 hours in the refrigerator (or rest overnight) to chill before slicing and serving.

Irish Teatime Bakewell Tart

Serves 6

This tart is a delicious classic dessert with a moist and heavenly filling, especially for almond flavor lovers, called Frangipane. Although the dessert originated in England, it is hugely popular in Ireland and is showcased in most Irish bakeries and cafes, or you may see it on the menu as part of an elegant afternoon tea in a Castle or Stately home.

The almond flour, combined with the added layer of raspberry jam, make it a very moist cake and the perfect complement to an Irish cup of tea! If you want to be truly authentic, serve the tea strong with a good dash of milk and a spoonful of sugar.

PASTRY INGREDIENTS

1⅔ cups (7 ounces) of flour (I use equal parts cake flour to all purpose)
¼ cup of confectioners' sugar
4 ounces cold unsalted butter
1 egg yolk
2 tablespoons ice water
Pinch of salt

FILLING

6 tablespoons of raspberry jam

FRANGIPANE INGREDIENTS

4 ounces unsalted butter (room temperature)
½ cup of granulated sugar
1¼ cup (120 g) almond flour
¼ cup (28 g) of cake flour
¼ teaspoon salt
1 egg (and 1 egg yolk)
1 teaspoon almond extract
1 teaspoon vanilla extract

TOPPING

½ cup of flaked almonds

HOW TO MAKE

1. Grease a standard 9-inch fluted tin pan.

2. To make the pastry, sieve the flour and sugar together. Rub in the butter until it resembles breadcrumbs. Using a knife, stir in the egg yolk and water to form a dough. Roll the dough out on a lightly floured surface large enough to slightly hang over the edges of the greased fluted tin. Use a knife to trim the edges and refrigerate for 30 minutes.

3. Preheat the oven to 400°F. Line the tin with parchment and baking beans, and blind bake the crust for the first 15 minutes. Remove the parchment and beans and bake for 5 more minutes to bake center of the pastry. Remove from the oven and set aside to cool.

4. To make the frangipane, beat the butter and sugar together until light and fluffy, and then beat in the egg and egg yolk and almond and vanilla essence. Fold in the almond flour and the cake flour.

5. Spread the jam over the base of the tart with the back of a spoon. Spoon the frangipane cake filling on top and then top with the flaked almonds.

6. Bake for 35–40 minutes until golden brown and firm to the touch.

Chapter Four

Old Traditions in a New Land

Irish fusion recipes as we put down roots

Despite the hardships of immigrant life for the Irish in America, the influence of millions of Scots-Irish, followed by Gaelic Irish settlers has changed the American culture over time. Irish music, phrases and culture have so fused into American culture that it is sometimes almost invisible. Consider bluegrass and country music for example. Many of the rhythms of American music have a direct link to the Irish who settled in Appalachia but the centuries since have moved the fusion to a place that is unique.

Fusion of the old with the new has been an exciting journey for me as I put down roots and learned to blend the Irish food traditions I knew so well, with the influences all around me in my new American home.

Sooner or later, we all learn to settle down.

Settling Down and Settling In

John and Etta tied the knot on June 1899 and the occasion is marked by a golden watch locket engraved with their initials that is still a treasured family heirloom. Looking at Etta's face in their wedding portrait, I can feel the determination, the drive, the value of hard work that has been the hallmark of the Irish in America.

The happy couple settled in the East Summerville neighborhood of Boston where John continued to work as a self-employed carpenter, working on new construction as many of the young Irish men did in those days. Etta became a homemaker, and before long they were expecting their first child, my grandfather; John McNeill.

Between 1900 and 1915, more than 15 million immigrants arrived in the United States. This was equivalent

to the number of immigrants who had arrived in the previous 40 years, and so it was a time of great change. America was that place of opportunity, especially those who could offer skilled professions such as carpentry, metal working or textile production. It was a competitive time, but there was plenty of work for those with skill and determination.

Etta no doubt experimented in the kitchen with new ingredients found in America and put her own spin on traditional Irish recipes as I did a century later. The Boston Cooking School produced the groundbreaking *Fannie Farmer Cookbook* in 1896, showing readers how to set a table for a proper teas and dinners of the time. I have a precious copy from that era, and the recipes and entertaining tips are such a window into haute culture of that Titanic era. One such recipe, for example, shows home cooks how to make rolled wafers and tie them in bundles of three with baby ribbon for dessert. It was a time of elegance with the larger homes having cooks and lady maids to keep up with the pressure to perform.

After the struggle of those early years as Irish immigrants, Etta and John had now settled down. Had a home of their own and a baby on the way. Things seemed to be going so well as the nineteenth century gave way to the twentieth with all its hopes and dreams—until a letter arrived from Ireland. A letter that would change their destiny once more. A letter from home.

A Food Fusion of Old with New

Many of the fusion recipes in this chapter are a blend of traditional Irish and the American way of doing things that I have discovered living here, incorporating familiar flavors from Ireland with the newfound flavors of the deep South.

Over 10 years ago, I founded my company; Shamrock and Peach Foods, providing intimate catering events throughout the South, and cooking has given me the opportunity to travel and soak in the culture. I have hosted dinner parties for both the Irish and British Consulate Generals, I have cooked for Getty Music in Nashville and toured Florida with Publix Cooking Schools and Kerrygold. I cooked at Disney's Food and Wine exhibition in Epcot, represented Tourism Ireland in Atlanta, and even had the wonderful opportunity to cook at the James Beard House in New York with my dear friends, chef Noel McMeel and Margaret Johnston.

Cooking with culture is fun, and food fusion is a wonderful journey of discovery. So let me invite you to explore this unique pairing with some wonderful fusion recipes.

OLD TRADITIONS IN A NEW LAND

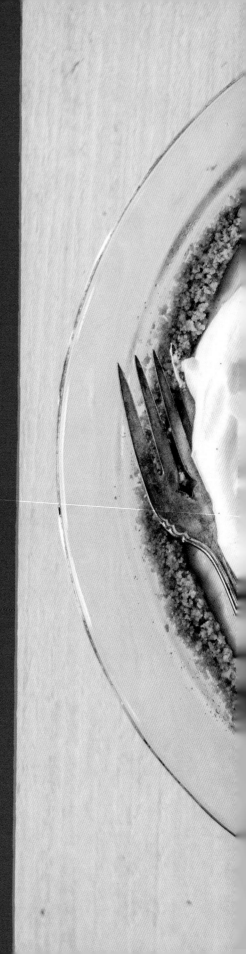

CHAPTER FOUR
Irish Fusion Foods

Coconut and Vanilla Bean Cream Pie
(page 116)

Collard Greens Salad with Roasted Sweet Potato & Seed Brittle

Collard greens are in the same cabbage family as spring greens, turnip greens and kale and are a brilliant source of vitamin C. In the American South, slow cooked, soft collard greens are considered a Southern delicacy, and can be found on the menus of many Southern inspired restaurants and barbecue joints.

After years of living in the American South, I have found these spicy and hearty greens to be delicious in salads and they stand up to lots of strong flavors such as garlic. Other hearty leafy greens that would make great substitutes for collards include Swiss chard, mustard greens, black kale, or beet greens.

SWEET POTATOES INGREDIENTS

2 medium sweet potatoes (peeled and diced)
2 tablespoons olive oil
8 cups collard greens (hard stalks removed/thinly sliced in ribbons)
½ cup dried cherries or cranberries

SEED BRITTLE INGREDIENTS

2 tablespoons pumpkin seeds
2 tablespoons sunflower seeds
1 tablespoon sesame seeds
1 teaspoon Irish butter (melted)
1½ tablespoons raw honey
Pinch of kosher salt

GARLIC VINAIGRETTE INGREDIENTS

3 tablespoons cider vinegar
1 clove of garlic (crushed)
1 tablespoon course Dijon mustard
2 teaspoons honey
½ cup of olive oil
Kosher salt
Freshly milled black pepper

HOW TO MAKE

1. Preheat the oven to 350°F. Toss the sweet potatoes in olive oil and bake for 15 minutes until they begin to brown on the edges. Remove from the oven and cool.

2. To make the vinaigrette, whisk the apple cider vinegar, garlic, mustard, and honey and then slowly incorporate the olive oil. Season with salt and pepper.

3. To make the harvest seed crunch, preheat the oven to 350°F. Whisk the melted butter and honey together. On a parchment lined baking sheet, toss the seeds with the butter and raw honey. Toast the seeds for 10–12 minutes and then stir and bake for a further few minutes until they are golden brown and aromatic. Remove from the oven and allow seeds to cool completely.

4. To shred the collards greens, remove the hard stalk in the center and then roll in a cigar shape and slice into ribbons.

5. Toss the shredded greens in about ½ cup of the vinaigrette and allow marinating and softening the greens for about 10 minutes. Fold in the dried cranberries, additional vinaigrette and season with a little more kosher salt and pepper to taste.

6. To serve the salad, break up the seed brittle and sprinkle over the top of the greens.

Lentil & Butternut Squash Soup

Serves 4–6

Butternut squash is native to the New World, a vegetable that would have been cultivated by the native Americans before European settlers ever settled on these shores and has wonderful orange flesh and a sweet nutty taste, just like a pumpkin. Endlessly fascinating to Irish immigrants like me.

Carrot and Lentil soup is a classic combination in Ireland, with the stock often made using a ham bone that gives it a lovely sweet and smokey flavor. My fusion here substitutes the butternut squash for the carrots and adds some spicy flavors at the end to round everything off and create a classic soup with an American twist.

SOUP INGREDIENTS

1 medium onion (finely chopped)
2 tablespoons butter
2 teaspoons red Thai curry paste
1 tablespoon fresh root ginger (peeled and grated)
2 cloves of garlic (crushed)
10.5 ounces (1½ cups) lentils (rinsed and soaked)
3 pints (6 cups) ham or vegetable stock
1½ pounds of butternut squash (peeled, seeded, and diced)
1 tablespoon brown sugar
1 teaspoon fine sea salt
Dash of freshly ground black pepper

GARNISH INGREDIENTS

3-4 tablespoons crème fraiche
Pinch of kosher salt
Squeeze of lemon juice

HOW TO MAKE

1. Soak the lentils for a few hours beforehand to remove any foreign materials.

2. Melt the butter in a large saucepan on medium heat and sauté the onions until fragrant and translucent.

3. Add the curry powder and stir until fragrant.

4. Stir in the root ginger and garlic and sauté just for a minute.

5. Add the stock, drained lentils, butternut squash, brown sugar, salt, pepper.

6. Bring to a boil and then reduce the heat. Cover and simmer for 30 minutes, stirring occasionally until the lentils are soft.

7. Purée the soup with a food mill or liquidize in a blender.

8. Transfer the soup to a saucepan and slowly heat through. Taste to adjust seasoning.

9. Prepare the garnish by blending a little kosher salt with lemon juice, mixing them into the crème fraiche.

10. Serve the soup in warmed bowls with a dollop of the crème fraiche mixture.

Simply Southern Cheese Spreads

Each Recipe Serves 4–6

When entertaining, a welcome appetizer sets the mood as the guests mingle and move around a welcome appetizer, or cheese board. Everyone just enjoys a delicious cheese spread with crispy crackers, vegetable crudes or artisan breads on such occasions.

Both cheese spreads here are Southern inspired recipes that I have adapted over the years for my catering events which use flavorful grass-fed Irish cheeses. The cheddar by Joe Hegarty is the stuff that would make you want to walk over hot coals to taste it and Teresa Roche's Kylemore cheese is the only Alpine style farmhouse cheese made in Ireland. They are both the inspiration for these dips. Make ahead of time and chill.

Southland Pimento Cheese

PIMENTO CHEESE INGREDIENTS	HOW TO MAKE
14 ounces Irish cheddar cheese (grated) 7 ounces jar of roasted piquillo red peppers 4 tablespoons chives (finely chopped) ½ cup mayonnaise 3 tablespoons juice from drained red piquillo peppers 3 tablespoons lemon juice 8 drops McIlhenny's tabasco hot sauce ½ teaspoon siracha ½ teaspoon freshly milled black pepper 1 clove garlic (crushed)	1. Grate the cheese by hand or using a food processor cheese cutting blade. 2. Drain the peppers from the jar, reserving 3 tablespoons of the liquid before finely chopping. 3. Finely chop the chives or snip with kitchen scissors. 4. Combine the mayonnaise, lemon juice, garlic, reserved liquid from peppers and add to the grated cheese. Add the Tabasco, smoked paprika and ground black pepper.

Almond, Bacon & Cheese

ALMOND, BACON, CHEESE INGREDIENTS	HOW TO MAKE
2 cups of Irish Swiss Cheese (grated) 1 cup of mayonnaise ⅓ cup slivered almonds (toasted) 6 strips of bacon (cooked until crispy and chopped) 2 green onions (finely sliced) 2 cloves of garlic (minced)	1. Combine all the ingredients together and stir to combine. Cover and refrigerate until ready to serve. 2. Serve room temperature with crackers and vegetable crudités.

Soft Sweet Potato Biscuits with Country Ham Spread

Serves 4–6

Warm soft sweet potato biscuits with salty country ham are a taste of American fusion to me. My Irish roots make me think of savory scones and how immigrants fused old world techniques to create new 'biscuits' we all crave.

These are lovely for as part of an appetizer cocktail party or for a brunch with a slice of bacon, egg, and avocado.

HAM SALAD INGREDIENTS

1¼ cups country ham (finely diced or whirled in the processor)
½ cup chopped sweet pickle
½ cup diced celery
1 tablespoon spicy wholegrain mustard
¼ cup mayonnaise
2 tablespoons chopped chives
(Optional toppings: avocado, bacon, fried egg)

BISCUITS INGREDIENTS

1¾ cups all-purpose flour
1 tablespoon sugar
2½ teaspoons baking powder
½ teaspoons baking soda
7 tablespoons shortening (chilled)
1⅓ cups cooked sweet potatoes (3 medium size sweet potatoes)
½ cup buttermilk (to mix)

HOW TO MAKE

1. To make the ham salad, combine the country ham, sweet pickle, celery, mayonnaise, spicy wholegrain mustard together in a small bowl.

2. To make the biscuits, preheat the oven to 425°F.

3. Sift the flour, baking powder, baking soda and sugar into a large bowl. Rub in the shortening until the mixture resembles breadcrumbs. Combine the buttermilk and sweet potatoes stirring with a knife to incorporate. Roll the dough to ¾-inch thickness and then cut with a medium size biscuit cutter. Bake the biscuits for 15–18 minutes until they are golden brown.

4. To assemble the biscuits, cut each one in half and spread a little butter with a knife and top with your favorite toppings (bacon, avocado, egg, and ham salad)!

Date & Pecan Wholemeal Scones

Scones served with a cup of tea were an important part of hospitality growing up in Ireland. Often "elevenses," a break around 11 in the morning, would include a homemade scone with Irish butter, jam and cream.

This family recipe uses wholegrains that offer the best nutritional choice. The trick to making scones is to work the butter in to the grains with your fingers or a knife and not overwork the dough.

BUTTERMILK SCONE INGREDIENTS

2¾ cups whole meal flour
1 cup quick oats (plus 2 tablespoons to scatter on top)
⅓ cup wheat germ
2½ teaspoons baking powder
1 teaspoon baking soda
1 tablespoon fine granulated sugar
½ cup butter
2 eggs (beaten)
¾ cup buttermilk
1 tablespoon treacle or molasses
½ cup of dates (roughly chopped)
⅓ cup pecans (toasted)
1 egg beaten with 1 tablespoon of water to glaze
Pinch of salt

HOW TO MAKE

1. Preheat the oven to 425°F.

2. Prepare the fresh dates by cutting them in half lengthwise and removing the seed. Chop the dates and set them aside.

3. Toast the pecans for 3–4 minutes in the oven. Set the pecans aside to cool.

4. Sift together the flour, sugar, and baking soda in a bowl. Stir in the oats.

5. Rub the butter into the mixture with your fingers until it resembles coarse crumbs. Stir in the prepared pecans and dates.

6. Make a well in the center of dry mixture then set aside.

7. In another bowl, combine the egg and buttermilk then fold all at once into the dry mixture.

8. Stir until moistened then knead 3 or 4 times to create the dough.

9. Use a floured rolling pin to flatten the dough to measure about 1-inch in height.

10. Cut scones using a 1½-inch fluted pastry or cookie cutter and place each cutout on a large baking pan. Brush the tops with egg glaze using a pastry brush and scatter a few old-fashioned oats on top.

11. Bake for 18–20 minutes until the scones are a light golden brown, turning the pan around halfway through baking time to ensure evenness.

Lemon Emerald Chicken

Roasted chicken is a family weeknight favorite, and when paired with this wonderful, nutty pesto it becomes a knockout winner. The sauce is a vibrant emerald, green color, the kale is peppery, and the basil is aromatic and sweet!

In this recipe, I use Lacinato kale (also known as Black, Dinosaur or Tuscan kale) because it is slightly sweeter than Curly kale. To spatchcock a chicken, or butterfly it, remove the backbone for a speedier way of enjoying dinner grilled or in the skillet.

CHICKEN MARINADE INGREDIENTS

5 tablespoons olive oil
1 lemon (3 tablespoons lemon juice and 3 slices)
3 cloves of garlic (crushed)
3 tablespoons mixed herbs (rosemary and parsley)

CHICKEN INGREDIENTS

2 tablespoons olive oil
Coarse salt and freshly ground pepper
3 pounds chicken (spatchcock)

KALE & WALNUT PESTO INGREDIENTS

½ cup walnuts (toasted with skins removed)
4 garlic cloves (roasted with the skins removed)
¼ cup Parmesan Reggiano cheese
½ teaspoon salt and freshly ground black pepper
2 cups chopped kale (rough center stalks and
    stems removed)
1 handful of basil (about 1 cup)
3 tablespoons lemon juice
Zest of one lemon
4 tablespoons water
½ cup olive oil

HOW TO MAKE

1. Preheat the oven to 400°F.

2. In a bowl stir the oil, lemon juice, garlic, and herbs together. Pierce the chicken with a fork and then pour the marinade on top. Allow the chicken to marinade for at least 20 minutes or overnight to let the flavors infuse. Place the chicken in a large skillet if roasting (or on a medium high grill). Drizzle with a little extra olive oil and season with salt and pepper skin side up and place the sliced lemons on top. Roast for 60–75 minutes, or until the skin is crispy.

3. To make the kale pesto, preheat the oven to 350°F and bake the walnuts for 6 minutes until they are fragrant and golden. Let them cool briefly and remove the skins by rubbing a few of them at a time between two dish towels.

4. In a large skillet, sauté the kale in 1 tablespoon of olive oil for 30 seconds and sprinkle over 2 tablespoons of water to wilt for 1 minute. Remove kale from heat and set aside to keep its vibrant green color.

5. In a food processor blend the walnuts, garlic, cheese and salt and pepper. Add the kale, basil and lemon juice and water. While the processor is moving, drizzle in the olive oil. Taste to adjust the seasoning or add a little more water if needed.

6. Drizzle the pesto over the warm chicken and enjoy!

Southern Summer Solstice Salad

My family, like many Irish families, grew greenhouse tomatoes and cucumbers that we always enjoyed by making soups and salads in the summer months. When I moved to the United States, I was introduced to the concept of adding the delicious flavors of peaches and watermelon to the Irish classic summer cucumber and tomato salads I knew so well, and I just love the addition of those fresh extra flavors.

One of my favorite summer road trips is to drive to the farms of South Georgia to buy watermelons and peaches to make this salad a true celebration of summer's bounty.

SALAD INGREDIENTS

1 pound of peaches (peeled and sliced in wedges)
1 pound heirloom tomatoes (cut into 1-inch chunks)
1 English cucumber (skin removed, halved lengthwise and sliced)
1 pound watermelon (skin remove and sliced in cubes)
12 basil leaves (torn)
4 ounces feta cheese (crumbled)

LEMON & MINT VINEGAR DRESSING

2 tablespoons lemon juice with zest of one lemon
1 tablespoon white wine vinegar
⅓ cup of shallots (minced)
5 tablespoons olive oil
Kosher salt and freshly ground black pepper
12 mint leaves (chopped)

HOW TO MAKE

1. In a bowl whisk together the shallots, lemon juice and zest and the white wine vinegar. Whisk in the olive oil in a slow and steady stream. Stir in the mint, and season with salt and pepper, and set aside.

2. Prepare the cucumbers and toss them in half of the lemon and mint vinegar dressing.

3. Slice the peaches, tomatoes and watermelon and toss them in the remaining lemon vinegar dressing.

4. To assemble the salad, combine the peaches, tomatoes, and the cucumber on a large platter. Sprinkle over the feta cheese, and then the basil.

Smothered Pork Chops with Orange & Ginger

In the American South pork chops are a family weeknight meal, often pan fried and smothered in a delicious and incredibly rich onion gravy. Growing up, my Irish mother used to serve our family smothered pork chops with an orange and ginger sauce for a simple weeknight meal.

My American fusion on my mother's family recipe is inspired by the time I lived in New England, and the vibrant red flooded fields of Cranberries I got to see! The richness of the pork and sweetness of the orange is tempered by the tartness of the cranberries, each one complimenting the other.

PORK CHOP INGREDIENTS

4 (1¼-inch thick) pork chops (room temperature)
2 tablespoons orange juice (to marinade)
kosher salt and pepper
3 tablespoons all-purpose flour
1 teaspoon ground ginger
2 tablespoons vegetable oil

ORANGE SAUCE INGREDIENTS

2 teaspoons grated fresh ginger
2 ounces (¼ cup) of chicken stock
4 ounces (1 cup) fresh cranberries
6 slices of orange (for garnish)
Kosher salt and pepper
2 tablespoons honey
1 clove garlic (crushed)
1 teaspoon soy sauce
1⅓ cups freshly squeezed orange juice
1½ teaspoons of orange zest
3 tablespoons flour
5 tablespoons butter

SOY GINGER DRIZZLE INGREDIENTS

2 teaspoons freshly grated ginger
3 tablespoons light soy sauce
2 tablespoons Grand Marnier
1 tablespoon water
1 tablespoon honey

HOW TO MAKE

1. Marinate the chops for 20 minutes in orange juice. Preheat oven to 400°F.

2. Combine the flour and ginger. Season pork chops with salt and pepper and then coat in the flour and ginger mixture.

3. Heat the oil in a large skillet and sear seasoned pork chops on high heat until both sides are and golden brown (about 2–3 minutes on each side).

4. Remove the pork chops from the pan and set aside in a clean skillet.

5. Zest and squeeze oranges. Add the butter to the pan and melt before adding the remaining 3 tablespoons of flour. Stir together and cook for about 1 minute, as you would do when making a roux, before adding orange juice, zest, ginger, garlic, soy sauce, stock and honey. Season with salt and pepper.

6. Strain sauce over pork chops. Stir in cranberries and bake for a further 18–20 minutes or until the internal temperature is 140°F and the chops are firm to the touch. Allow the chops to rest for 5 minutes before serving.

7. To make the soy ginger sauce, combine the soy sauce, ginger, water, Grand Marnier, and honey together in a blender.

8. To serve, place the pork chop in the center of each plate and spoon the orange cranberry sauce on top. Drizzle a little of the ginger soy sauce, and garnish with a slice of twisted orange.

Low Country Watermelon Pickles

Preserving is a taste of remembrance of the abundance of summer, and it is an economical way to preserve summer vegetables and fruits in the winter months. My grandmother used to make a pickled relish from her homegrown cabbage, peppers and onions and there was always so much pride of making something with a relatively low cost.

Early immigrants to America loved traveling with pickled foods because they could survive the long journeys. The Scots-Irish, famously known for their thriftiness, appreciate being able to make something good out of what we would otherwise throw away, and the same is true here with a Low Country recipe that uses the rind of the watermelon that would in most cases just be thrown away.

WATERMELON PICKLE INGREDIENTS

1 pound of watermelon rind (hard green skin removed)

SOAKING INGREDIENTS

3 tablespoons coarse salt
6 cups of water

BRINE INGREDIENTS

1½ cups apple cider vinegar
1½ cups sugar
½ lemon (thinly sliced)
1 teaspoon fresh ginger (minced)
1 cinnamon stick (crushed)
1 teaspoon all spice berries (crushed)

HOW TO MAKE

1. To prepare the watermelon rind, remove the hard-green skin, and take off almost all the red watermelon meat. Cut the rind in to 1½-inch length pieces.

2. Combine the salt and water in a medium size bowl and add the rind to the brine. Soak for several hours or overnight to soften the rind.

3. In a saucepan combine the apple cider vinegar, water, sugar, and spices and bring to a boil stirring until the sugar has dissolved.

4. Drain the watermelon rinds from the overnight soak and rinse under running water. Place the drained watermelon in a saucepan, cover with water and simmer for 10 minutes until the rind has softened and is translucent.

5. Drain the watermelon rind and then pour the prepared pickling brine on top. Simmer the rind and bring for another 15 minutes.

6. Prepare sterilized jars. Using a slotted spoon add the watermelon rinds to the jars, and then pour the unstrained syrup to fill the jars. Leaving a ¼-inch space before canning!

Sweet & Spicy Wheat Beer Wings

Serves 6

Irish Pub food is famous throughout the world and chicken wings and beer must be one of the most loved fusion foods available in the United States, especially when watching sporting events.

The bitter hoppy taste of the beer with sweet honey and a touch of spice is such a perfect combination with a pint of beer and improved with great company!

WINGS MARINADE INGREDIENTS

3 pounds of chicken wings
1 bottle of Harp Irish Beer (12 ounces)
3 cloves of garlic (crushed)
1 tablespoon freshly grated stem ginger
⅓ cup hot sriracha chili sauce
2 tablespoons olive oil
2 tablespoons lemon juice
¼ cup soy sauce

GLAZE INGREDIENTS

¼ cup honey
¼ cup spring onions (thinly sliced)
1 tablespoon fresh chili (finely chopped for garnish)

HOW TO MAKE

1. Combine the beer, garlic, ginger, sriracha, lemon juice, olive oil and soy sauce. Pour half of the marinate over the chicken and reserve the other half for later.

2. Allow the chicken to marinate for at least 30 minutes. Remove the chicken from the marinade.

3. Preheat the oven to 500°F.

4. Place the chicken on a large baking tray to roast and bake for 45 minutes until the skin is crispy.

5. While the wings are in the oven place the remaining marinate into a small saucepan and reduce it by about 50 percent. Whisk in the honey and half of the spring onions.

6. Preheat the grill to medium high.

7. Remove the wings from the roasting pan and transfer to the grill to crisp and char for a few minutes.

8. Brush the wings with the glaze.

9. To serve, sprinkle the reserved spring onions and fresh chili over the wings.

Coconut & Vanilla Bean Cream Pie

There is something delightful about a homemade silky cream pie that delights the heart! When I smell the aroma of toasted coconut it reminds me of the little coconut haystack buns topped with a glace cherry, a special sweet treat from the Irish pantry! The natural exotic flavor of coconut is only intensified in this pie, with the addition of coconut milk made from juiced coconut meat and water.

COCONUT CRUST INGREDIENTS

1½ cups (225 g) digestive biscuits/graham crackers
½ cup sweetened coconut
1 tablespoon sugar
6 tablespoons unsalted butter (melted)

FOR THE COCONUT FILLING

13.5 ounces can of full fat coconut milk
1 cup whole milk
½ cup heavy whipping cream
3 large eggs (beaten)
¾ cup sugar
½ cup cornstarch
1½ cups sweetened coconut
1 vanilla bean (scraped to remove its seeds)
Pinch of salt

TOPPING INGREDIENTS

1 cup heavy whipping cream
2 tablespoons fine granulated sugar
1 teaspoon coconut extract
⅓ cup unsweetened coconut chips (toasted)

HOW TO MAKE

1. To make the crust, pulse preheat the oven to 350°F. Combine the cookies, coconut, and sugar together in the food processor to grind them up. Add the melted butter and pulse until incorporated. Press the mixture into a 9-inch pie dish, using the bottom of a flat measuring cup to make sure the crust is tight and compact. Bake the crust for 7–10 minutes and then set aside to cool.

2. To make the coconut custard, add the coconut milk, milk, cream, and sugar to a medium saucepan. Add the vanilla bean seeds and whisk to combine (add the vanilla bean to infuse flavor). Simmer gently on a low heat for a few minutes until the sugar has dissolved. Whisk the eggs and cornstarch together in a small bowl to form a paste. Add the milk mixture slowly to temper the eggs, whisking until combined. Strain the mixture back into the saucepan, discarding the vanilla bean and cook the custard for 5–7 minutes, stirring continuously until it has thickened. Stir in the sweetened coconut, and then pour the custard over the cooled cookie crumb base. Set aside to cool completely.

3. To make the topping, whip the cream, sugar, and coconut extract together in an electric mixer until stiff peaks form. Spoon the cream over the coconut custard and refrigerate for several hours to set (the pie is even better the next day for a firmly set crust).

4. To decorate the pie, preheat the oven to 375°F. Place the unsweetened coconut on a baking tray and toast for 4 minutes or until golden and fragrant. Cool and then sprinkle over the pie and serve!

Nana Custard Pudding in a Jar

Serves 6

There seems to be an army of custard trifle recipes both in Ireland and America, with every family having their own favorite. This quirky version is affectionately called Nana Pudding, and when I serve it in a jar like this, it creates a fun moment at any gathering.

The fresh bananas are enveloped in the most delicious vanilla custard, the soft vanilla base and topped with pillowy meringue, but one thing that unites us all, is that one spoonful is never enough!

PUDDING INGREDIENTS

1¾ cup of sugar
6 eggs (separated)
½ cup all-purpose flour
3 cups of whole milk
1 teaspoon vanilla
Pinch of fine sea salt

BASE INGREDIENTS

¼ cup of butter
11 ounces of Nilla wafers (vanilla cookies)
5 medium ripe bananas

HOW TO MAKE

1. To make the pudding beat the egg yolks and milk together and blend with the flour, 1¼ cup sugar and salt on top of a double boiler.

2. Cook slowly stirring all the time on medium low heat for 8–10 minutes or until the custard has thickened. Remove from the heat and stir in the vanilla and whisk in the butter.

3. Begin to layer the pudding in 6 one-cup size jars by spreading a small layer of the pudding followed by the vanilla wafers, layer of sliced bananas and then repeating the layers ending with the custard.

4. Preheat the oven to 325°F.

5. To make the meringue, beat the egg whites until soft peaks form and then gradually add the remaining ½ cup of sugar 1 teaspoon at a time until the meringue is stiff.

6. Spoon meringue on top of the pudding and bake for 12–15 minutes or until the meringue is toasted and golden brown.

7. Serve the pudding warm or cold.

Eastward Bound

Discovering modern Irish foods in a changing world

For centuries, the Irish American experience was based on an east to west migration. Immigrants went to America and almost never returned home. The reasons were almost always economic. It was simply too arduous and too expensive to make the journey. Many associated the old country with poverty and hardship and were eager to leave that behind in pursuit of prosperity.

That experience however has changed in the 21st century. A prosperous Ireland and an American sense of curiosity have turned the tables. Now more Americans are traveling to the Celtic lands than ever before and are discovering a world of beauty, culture, and wonderful food. Gone are the bland meals of boiled potatoes, often overcooked vegetables, and meat to be replaced with a new appreciation of the quality of the meat reared on lush green fields, the milk from those happy cows, goats and sheep, the fish, and shellfish from the pristine waters of the Atlantic Ocean and the traditional breads and bakes. A return to Ireland.

The Letter from Home

In 1900, a letter from Ireland to America was a rare and precious thing, and for Etta and John they had received a letter that was going to change their lives forever. An uncle of John's had sadly died, but he had left him a farm in the rolling hills of County Down in Ireland. As if by a miracle, they now had land. They had an unexpected opportunity and a return to Ireland had appeared as if from nowhere.

John and Etta had left Ireland for the dream that was America. They had meager prospects in Ireland, but this letter changed everything. An uncle, who had died childless leaving them this land had opened a new world once more.

Few immigrants ever returned, and reverse immigration was unheard of in those days, but here they were. The American journey was exciting, but as all Irish people will tell you, the prospect of land of your own is too good to miss so John and Etta did the unthinkable. They packed up. They sold what they had, and they returned to Ireland. My grandfather was not destined to be born in New England after all, but in Auglishnafin in County Down.

Some months later when Etta returned to Ireland, bringing with her all her influences and experiences from America, she was the talk of the village. They had resources to build their own home on the new land, and that house is still standing today. They were the first in their area to own their own car, and all of this was made possible by money they had earned in America.

That spirit of elegant hospitality that Etta learned in the big houses of New England, continued throughout her life. She would pass this on to her children, and her grandchildren. And her granddaughter, my mother, would pass this onto me. The love of learning from other cultures and traditions; it is all part of the journey home!

Coming Full Circle

As if completing the circle once more, I now have the joy and privilege to bring many guests with me on multiple return journeys to Ireland with my travel company, also called *Shamrock and Peach*. My travel adventures evolved from my cooking adventures where my guests at events where eager to know more about where my food influences came from, and they were curious as a result to visit the Celtic lands of which I spoke so highly.

It is such a joy to bring my friends and guests with me to Ireland. To experience Irish beauty through the eyes of visitors who have never seen those magical landscapes or castles, is a thing to behold. So many American visitors express complete surprise at how wonderfully modern and alive Ireland is today. From the snug pubs of the cities, quirky bed and breakfasts and boutique hotels to the elegant country houses and estates, my guests are always comparing their experiences of Ireland with their previous conceptions of what they thought it would have been like. The few who would have come back from journeys home in previous decades would still have come across often mediocre food in hotels. The ubiquitous cooked breakfast menu is now name-checked with local artisan producers. Some are still making the traditional sausages, bacon, and black pudding they always have, but a new breed of cheese makers, charcuterie producers and bakers are adding to the modern Irish food experience. It is not unusual to have a Waterford Blaa bread roll with chorizo made in Cork from the best Irish pork and free-range duck eggs for breakfast accompanied by loose leaf Irish Breakfast tea. Lunch could be a salad of goat cheese with organic leaves and a dressing made with balsamic vinegar infused with Armagh apples! To have such wonderful food and hospitality in such unique surroundings makes the long journey across the Atlantic so worthwhile.

Our small island, that survived the Irish famine, poverty and hardship with millions leaving her shores, is now welcoming her people home to a land of plenty, and a land of surprising elegance and sophistication.

So let me invite you on a journey of discovery here as we turn the page on misconceptions and find that Irish food is a wonderful thing.

Return with me to Ireland.

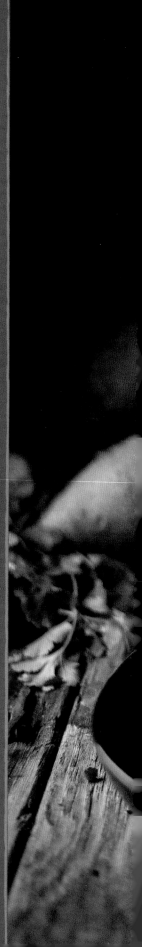

CHAPTER FIVE

Surprising Modern Irish Foods

Lime & Yogurt Sweet Potato Wedges
(page 127)

Irish Cheese Board
with Tomato Bacon Jam

Makes 2 cups of jam

In Ireland, our grass-fed livestock produces some of the finest milk that forms the basis for some of the finest cheeses in the world. Whilst visiting Ireland you may commonly be offered a dessert or a cheese board at the end of your meal and whilst charcuterie style boards are trending now, an Irish cheese board has never gone out of fashion.

For decades, the Republic was ahead of Northern Ireland in its cheese story. German and Dutch immigrants brought their cheese-making traditions including Silke Cropp from Corleggy in Cavan and Marian Roeleveld from Killeen in Galway. Now, Northern Ireland has caught up with Young Buck from Mike's Fancy Cheese and Ballylisk of Armagh among others.

To accompany, cheeses are often served with fine preserves, such as Erin Grove Preserves Fruits for Cheese in Sour Cherry and Black Pepper or Damson and Gin flavors, Pear and Walnut Chutney from Yellow Door in Portadown or this tomato bacon jam.

CHEESE SELECTION INGREDIENTS

Hard cheese (mature Irish cheddars, smoked cheddars, gouda)
Soft and semi soft cheese (goat and sheep cheese, Gubbeen cow's milk, Gurteen button)
Blue cheese (Cashel Blue, Crozier Blue, Wicklow Blue, Blue Rathgore)

BOARD INGREDIENTS

Rustic crackers such as Sheridan's, Robert Ditty's Oatcakes or Foods of Athenry toasts

BACON JAM INGREDIENTS

1 pound applewood smoked bacon (cut in to 1-inch pieces)
1½ cups red onion (1 large onion)
3 cloves of garlic
2½ ounces (⅓ cup) brown sugar
1 pound (2½ cups) of tomatoes
¼ cup brown sugar
2 tablespoons malt vinegar
1 teaspoon Worcestershire sauce
1 teaspoon smoked paprika
½ teaspoons kosher salt
¼ teaspoon black pepper

HOW TO MAKE

1. To make the tomato bacon jam cook the bacon in a skillet over medium heat until all the fat has rendered, and the bacon is crispy. Using a slotted spoon, transfer the bacon on to a plate lined with paper towels to drain. Drain some of the fat leaving 2 tablespoons in the pan, and then add the red onions with the brown sugar until they have caramelized.

2. Add the garlic and cook for one minute and then deglaze the pan with the vinegar, Worcestershire sauce scraping any brown bits. Season with the paprika, salt and pepper and cook on low for 8–10 minutes to reduce further until the consistency is syrupy. Stir in the bacon and cook for a few more minutes.

3. Allow the jam to cool before transferring to an airtight or sterilized jar.

4. To assemble arrange the cheeses and crackers on a slate or wooden board. Serve the tomato jam on the side, in a small bowl, with a serving spoon.

Ruby Rocket Salad

Serves 4–6

In Ireland, we call arugula "garden rocket." It is a trending spicy green that is part of the mustard family which grows prolifically in the summer months on Irish vegetable plots in back gardens. It may surprise you to see ingredients such as pomegranates and pistachios on an Irish menu, but this delicious combination pairs well with local fresh goat cheese, drizzled with maple pomegranate vinaigrette.

SALAD INGREDIENTS

8 cups baby arugula
1 pomegranate
4 ounces (½ cup) goat cheese (crumbled)

ROASTED PISTACHIO INGREDIENTS

¾ cup pistachio nuts

VINAIGRETTE INGREDIENTS

2 tablespoons pomegranate vinegar
  (or red wine vinegar)
1 tablespoon orange juice
2 tablespoons maple syrup
1 tablespoon Dijon mustard
½ teaspoon kosher salt
¼ teaspoon freshly ground pepper
½ cup olive oil

HOW TO MAKE

1. Preheat oven to 350°F. Place the pistachio nuts in a single layer on a baking sheet. Bake for 7–8 minutes or until they are lightly browned and fragrant. Check after the first 5 minutes and stir to prevent burning. Transfer the pistachios on to a towel and rub gently to remove the skins. Allow to cool.

2. To remove the seeds from the pomegranate, fill a small bowl with cold water. Cut the pomegranate in half and using a spoon or hands scrape out the seeds and then strain removing any pith.

3. To make the vinaigrette, whisk the pomegranate vinegar, orange juice, maple syrup, Dijon mustard together and then slowly whisk in the olive oil one tablespoon at a time until an emulsion form. Season with salt and pepper.

4. In a large bowl combine arugula, pomegranate seeds, goat cheese, and two thirds of the pistachio nuts and toss gently with about half of the vinaigrette.

5. To serve, place greens in the center of each plate or large bowl. Sprinkle a few extra pistachio nuts and pomegranate seeds (and serve a little more vinaigrette on the side).

Lime & Yogurt Sweet Potato Wedges

Serves 4–6

Irish cafes and restaurants these days are serving a wide selection of nutritious dishes. As well as white potato, that Ireland is commonly known for, there are many healthy alternatives.

It is not at all unusual to see sweet potato fries and spelt and quinoa salads offered as side dishes. Pulses, roots, and grains now come in all manner of ways. This colorful sweet potato side dish lends itself to outdoor barbecue dining, and it is served room temperature!

SWEET POTATO INGREDIENTS

2 pounds sweet potatoes (washed with skins on)
3 tablespoons coconut oil
¼ teaspoon of salt

LIME YOGURT INGREDIENTS

½ cup of full fat whole milk yogurt
4 tablespoons lime juice (one large lime)
1 garlic clove (crushed)
1 clove of garlic (crushed)
2 teaspoons raw honey
Zest from one lime
Good pinch of salt and freshly ground black pepper

GARNISH INGREDIENTS

3 tablespoons (2 red chili finely chopped)
¼ cup of cilantro (chopped)

HOW TO MAKE

1. Preheat the oven to 400°F.

2. Cut the sweet potatoes in to uniform size wedges with the skins on and then toss them in the coconut oil and salt and pepper.

3. Place the sweet potatoes on a large baking try and roast them for 35–40 minutes until they are crisp out the outside and soft in the center, checking halfway through and turning them so they do not burn.

4. To make the dressing whisk the crème fraiche/Greek yogurt with the fresh lime juice and zest, crushed garlic and salt and pepper.

Irish Soda Flat Bread Pie

Serves 4–6 (one 10-inch pizza)

This pie crust is an absolute revolution to make dinner for your family in a flash, with the added flavor twist of soda bread, a long favored Irish favorite. Sliced bread as you know it is actually a relatively recent thing in Ireland. Sodas were made on the griddle as the staple bread up until the 1960s.

Making the dough is effortless, and it can be rolled out easily. It is the sort of how make a busy housewife in two shakes of a lamb's tail.

Think of this as traditional Irish soda bread reimagined, and since it is leavened with baking soda instead of yeast, it never fails to produce a flakey crust. It is an economical meal, and a fun recipe to introduce kids to the kitchen.

PIZZA INGREDIENTS

1¾ cups plus 2 tablespoons all-purpose flour
1 teaspoon baking soda
1 cup buttermilk (just under a cup)
16 ounces store-bought tomato sauce (plus 2 tablespoons water) or homemade tomato sauce (see below)
Pinch of sea salt

TOPPINGS INGREDIENTS

¾ cup cheese (I like to use ½ cup mozzarella and ¼ cup Irish cheddar)
Salami (thinly sliced)
(Optional toppings ideas: basil, thinly sliced onions, red peppers, ham, olives, bacon)

SAUCE INGREDIENTS (IF NEEDED)

1 tablespoon olive oil
2 tablespoons onion (chopped)
2 cloves of garlic (crushed)
6 ounces can tomato paste
1 tablespoon mixed herbs (oregano, marjoram, rosemary)
1 tablespoon sugar
1 teaspoon sea salt
Pinch of baking soda
¼ teaspoon freshly ground black pepper

HOW TO MAKE

1. To make the pizza dough, preheat the oven to 375°F.

2. Measure the flour and salt into a large bowl and sieve in the baking soda.

3. Make a well in the center and slowly add in the buttermilk, using a knife to make a sticky dough.

4. Lightly flour a dry surface and transfer the dough from the bowl. Knead the dough gently, and roll with a rolling pin, and then press into a flat pizza tray.

5. Spread the tomato sauce over the pizza base. Place the meats and any vegetables next and finally top with the cheeses.

6. Bake for 20 minutes until the base is cooked through and the topping is golden brown.

7. For the optional homemade Tomato Sauce, cook the onion and garlic together with the olive oil for 2 minutes and then add the rest of the ingredients and simmer gently for 15 minutes.

Slow Braised Shoulder of Lamb Stew

⤳ *Serves 4–6* ⤵

Irish lamb is reared on the lush green grass of the Emerald Isle, but that grass is always supplemented by wild herbs and in the case of Achill Mountain lamb in mayo seaweed and machair grass which give a seaside seasoning to the sweet heather on the hilltops.

This is a delicious dish that works great with potatoes but can also be amazing over some spinach pasta for a new spin with a touch of Irish green!

This melt in your mouth cassoulet is cooked for a few hours to perfection using the shoulder of lamb that lends itself to slow cooking. The ponderous cooking method permeates the kitchen with comforting aromas and will have everyone asking for more.

LAMB CASSOULET INGREDIENTS

4 ounces apple wood smoked bacon (finely diced)
2–3 tablespoons olive oil
3 pounds of gigot shoulder of lamb (with the bone in)
1 cup onion finely chopped
1 cup of carrots finely diced
¾ cup celery finely diced
¾ cup red pepper chopped
1 tablespoon finely chopped rosemary
2 cloves of garlic (minced)
¾ red wine
2 tablespoons tomato paste
1 teaspoon sugar
1 (28-ounce) can tomatoes coarsely chopped with juices
¾ cup of chicken stock
Kosher salt and freshly ground black pepper

SUGGESTED SIDE INGREDIENTS

1 pound fresh spinach and basil pasta (cooked al dente)
Parmigiano Reggiano (freshly grated)

HOW TO MAKE

1. Preheat the oven to 275°F.

2. In a medium skillet, heat 4 tablespoons of oil on medium high heat. Add the smoked bacon to the pan and cook until it is crispy, and the fat has rendered. Remove from the pan with a slotted spoon, leaving 2 tablespoons of fat in the skillet to cook the lamb.

3. Season the lamb chops with salt and pepper and begin to cook in small batches to sear and brown, adding more olive oil as necessary. It is important to let the chops brown evenly and not steam.

4. When all the chops are browned, combine all the seared meat together in the skillet, and then add the onion stirring until they are lightly browned. Stir in the carrots celery, red pepper, garlic, and the rosemary and allow them to cook for 5 minutes.

5. Add the red wine and allow it to reduce for 5 minutes or so. Stir in the canned tomatoes, tomato purée, chicken stock, sugar. Taste to adjust seasoning adding a little more salt and freshly ground pepper.

6. Place in the oven and cook for 2½–3 hours until the meat is almost falling off the bone. Allow the lamb to cool to room temperature, and then remove the chops and cut all the meat away from the bones using a knife. Discard all the bones and add the lamb meat back into the cassoulet along with the reserved crispy bacon.

7. To serve, slowly heat up the cassoulet, stirring to heat through. Place the freshly cooked al dente pasta in the center of each bowl and spoon the cassoulet on top. Sprinkle over a little bit of finely grated Parmigiano-Reggiano cheese.

Roasted Red Beets Salad

Serves 4–6

Ireland today celebrates vibrant textures and bold natural colorful dishes, and restaurants throughout Ireland are offering so much color and flavor compared to years ago. Beets, like all root vegetables, thrive in our nutrient rich Irish soil and roasting them in this recipe intensives its sweetness.

It is a far cry from the days of pickled beetroots in vinegar which turned so many off this glorious vegetable for life!

The earthy beets pair well with the tanginess of the lemony crème fraiche, and sunflower seeds add a welcome crunch. Colorful and fun to add to any table as an interesting side and talking point.

BEET SALAD INGREDIENTS

1½ pounds beets (6 medium size beets)
½ red onion (thinly sliced)
3 tablespoons parsley (chopped)
Drizzle of good olive oil
Freshly ground pepper and salt

TOASTED SUNFLOWER SEEDS

3 tablespoons sunflower seeds
1 teaspoon olive oil
¼ teaspoon kosher salt

LEMON CRÈME FRAICHE

½ cup crème fraiche
2 tablespoons lemon juice (and zest of one lemon)

HOW TO MAKE

1. Preheat oven to 425°F.
2. Brush beets with olive oil and wrap in aluminum foil and set on a baking sheet to roast for 40 minutes.
3. Remove the beets from the oven to cool.
4. Place the sunflower seeds on a baking sheet and toss them with the olive oil and kosher salt and bake for 6–7 minutes until they are toasted and fragrant. Remove from the oven and cool.
5. Combine the crème fraiche, lemon juice and zest together.
6. Remove the beets from the aluminum foil and slice. Toss the beets in the lemon crème fraiche dressing. Stir in the chopped red onion, 2 teaspoons of the parsley and toasted sunflower seeds and season with salt and freshly ground pepper.
7. To serve, drizzle with olive oil and the remaining parsley.

Fennel & Blood Orange Salad

Serves 4–6

In the winter months when fewer fresh seasonal fruits are available, blood oranges are a welcome addition to the market basket. The vibrant crimson red color livens the senses and adding some of the juice into the vinaigrette makes the plate really pop. The licorice flavored crunch of the fennel pairs well with the salty cheese, and there is just enough sweetness in the honey vinaigrette to bring the salad together.

SALAD INGREDIENTS

3 medium blood oranges (peeled and sliced)
1 small fennel bulb (cleaned, trimmed, and sliced)
½ small red onion (very thinly sliced)
4 cups Friese lettuce (hand torn)
1½ ounces mature grass-fed cheddar (such as Dubliner Irish cheese shaved)

VINAIGRETTE INGREDIENTS

1½ tablespoons shallots (very finely diced)
2 tablespoons sherry vinegar
1½ teaspoons raw honey
1 tablespoon orange juice plus 1 teaspoon zest
6 tablespoons extra-virgin olive oil
Kosher salt and pepper

HOW TO MAKE

1. To prepare the oranges, cut off the top and the base of the oranges. Stand each piece of fruit upright and cut off the peel and pith with a large, serrated knife. Using a sharp knife, cut the orange horizontally in slices.

2. To make the vinaigrette, combine the shallots, vinegar, honey, orange juice and zest in a small bowl. Slowly whisk in the olive oil and season with salt and pepper. Refrigerate until ready to use (this can be prepared in advance).

3. To assemble, place the salad in a large bowl, and toss the fennel and Friese lettuce in the prepared vinaigrette.

4. Arrange the greens in the center of each plate, then add the orange segments and top with the shaved red onion and Dubliner cheese.

Armagh Apple & Thyme Chicken

Serves 4

When apples are in season at home in County Armagh, kitchen cooks throughout the land love to be inventive with how to combine apples with savory entrees to highlight our county's rich bounty of fruit.

The Irish whiskey adds a subtle layer of flavor without taking away from the apples and thyme, and the dish is finished with a crispy fried sage leaf, that adds a final touch of herby elegance. Altogether, a balanced and delicious dish from my home county.

APPLE CHICKEN INGREDIENTS

2 pounds chicken breast fillets pounded ½-inch thick
4 tablespoons butter
1 tablespoon oil
1 sprig of thyme
4 Granny Smith apples (peeled, cored, and cut into wedges)
3 tablespoons brown sugar
½ cup finely chopped
¼ cup of apple cider vinegar
¼ cup of chicken stock
⅓ cup Irish whiskey
1 cup heavy whipping cream
Fine sea salt and pepper

SAGE GARNISH INGREDIENTS

4 sage leaves
Olive oil to fry and course sea salt

HOW TO MAKE

1. Preheat oven to 350°F. Place chicken breasts between pieces of plastic wrap, and use a meat mallet, to pound them to ½-inch thick. Season chicken fillets with freshly ground pepper and sea salt.

2. Melt 2 tablespoons of the butter in a large skillet and add the apples and sugar. Sauté the apples for 6–8 minutes, or until they are slightly soft and have caramelized.

3. In a large new skillet, heat 1 tablespoon of oil with 1 tablespoon of butter and sprig of thyme to medium/high heat. Add the chicken breasts to the skillet, working in batches, cooking on both sides for 2 minutes to brown and sear. Transfer the chicken to a clean casserole dish.

4. In the same skillet that the chicken was seared, make the sauce by melting the remaining 1 tablespoon of butter. Add the shallots and cook until soft and translucent. Deglaze the pan with the Irish whiskey until it has reduced, and then add the apple cider and cream, and cook until the sauce has thickened. Taste to adjust seasoning with salt and pepper.

5. Pour the sauce all over the chicken, and then add the caramelized apples on top. Bake for a further 18–20 minutes, until the chicken is cooked. Remove from the oven and discard the thyme.

6. Sauté the sage leaves in hot oil for 2–3 seconds, then transfer to a plate with paper towels to drain. Sprinkle them with coarse sea salt.

7. To serve, place the chicken breast in the center of the plate and spoon the sauce over chicken breast and top with the apples. Finally garnish with a fried sage leaf.

Cauliflower Steaks
with Poached Lobster Tails

Cauliflower is always featured on the Irish table, usually playing the part of the favored side in our Sunday roast dinner, but I have taken it for a spin here that I think you will enjoy.

This humble versatile vegetable has a mellow flavor, that pairs well with cream and butter and in this dish, we elevate it to being the star of the show alongside our favorite crustacean. The biggest challenge is cutting the "steak" out of the head of a cauliflower, but the purée in this recipe insures nothing is wasted.

LOBSTER INGREDIENTS

4 freshwater rock lobsters
1 tablespoon of salt

TARRAGON SAUCE INGREDIENTS

1 tablespoon olive oil
1 cup of chopped onion
1¼ cups of chopped carrots (cleaned and scraped)
¾ cup of chopped celery (washed)
¼ cup of dry white wine
¾ cup of water
2 tablespoons tomato purée
2 tablespoons of tarragon (chopped)
2 tablespoons butter
2 tablespoons cream
4 cloves of garlic
Kosher salt and freshly ground black pepper

CAULIFLOWER STEAK INGREDIENTS

1 large cauliflower or two smaller cauliflowers
  (cut four steaks)
½ cup of butter

PURÉE INGREDIENTS

1 cup broken cauliflower pieces
½ cup of cream
Kosher salt and pepper

HOW TO MAKE

1. Prepare a large pot of boiling water for the lobster and an ice bath. Plunge the lobster tails in for 30 seconds until the tail turns pink and then place them into the ice bath. Let the lobster cool for a few minutes and then using scissors, cut down the center of the lobster and remove the meat. Place the meat in the refrigerator.

2. To make the sauce, place the olive oil in a pan and add the onion, carrots, and celery cooking until they are soft. Add the white wine and reduce. Add the water and tomato purée and cook until the liquid has reduced by half. Remove from the heat, liquidize, and then strain the sauce.

3. To prepare the cauliflower, slice the steaks directly through the stem, making slabs that are ¾-inch thick, and keep the smaller pieces for the purée. Blanch the larger pieces in a small pot of boiling water and then plunge into an ice bath.

4. To make the cauliflower purée, chop up all the remaining broken pieces and place them in a small pot with a little water to cover and salt. Cook until most of the water has evaporated and then stir in the cream and cook for a few more minutes. Remove from the heat and the purée in liquidizer or Vitamix.

5. Remove the lobster tails from the refrigerator and bring a large pot of salted water to a boil. Poach the lobster for 4 minutes. Allow to rest for a few minutes.

6. To serve the dish, reheat the vegetable butter sauce and stir in the tarragon, cooking for 1 minute. Lightly brown the cauliflower steaks in butter and then arrange it around the outside of each plate. Place the cauliflower purée in the center with the poached lobster on top and then pour the butter sauce over and serve right away.

Shaved Brussels Sprouts with a Citrus Vinaigrette

Serves 4–6

Unlike the traditional boiled Brussels sprouts associated with the holiday turkey dinner table, this hearty raw salad is flavor packed with fresh and crunchy sprouts that absorb the delicious citrus garlic vinaigrette.

The raw Brussels sprouts also give the salad a welcome crunch, in addition to the toasted almonds add crispy bacon. This Brussels sprout salad makes a healthy lunch, or it can be served as a lively side dish.

SALAD INGREDIENTS

6 cups (16 ounces) of shaved Brussels sprouts (shaved)
6 slices of bacon (cooked and crumbled)
½ cup silvered almonds (toasted and roughly chopped)
¼ cup cranberries (chopped)
⅓ cup of Pecorino-Romano cheese (shaved)
Kosher salt and pepper

VINAIGRETTE INGREDIENTS

2 tablespoons fresh lemon
1 tablespoon fresh orange juice
1 tablespoon of maple syrup
2 cloves of garlic (minced)
½ teaspoon kosher salt
⅛ teaspoon ground black pepper
⅓ cup olive oil

HOW TO MAKE

1. Preheat the oven to 400°F. Cook the bacon on a baking sheet in the oven until crispy. Drain the bacon on paper towels.

2. While the oven is hot, place the almonds on a clean baking sheet and roast of 5 minutes until they are golden brown and fragrant.

3. To make the vinaigrette, whisk together the lemon and orange juice, garlic, and maple syrup and in a large salad bowl, and then add the olive oil in a slow steady stream. Season with salt and pepper and set aside.

4. Use a mandolin to carefully shave the Brussels sprouts stopping at the hard stems and discarding. You can also cut the hard stems off the Brussels sprouts and use the slicing attachment in your food processor. Rinse the Brussels sprouts under running water to ensure they are completely clean and then dry them well.

5. To assemble the salad, place the shaved Brussels sprouts in the salad bowl with the vinaigrette and then add the crumbled cooked bacon, toasted almonds, cranberries, and Pecorino-Romano Cheese and toss all the ingredients together.

Bold Buttermilk
& Vanilla Cream Pudding

Serves 4

There is nothing better than smooth and light thickened cream combined with cultured buttermilk which has been a favored food and drink in Ireland for thousands of years, combine this with all the amazing seasonal fruits, such as summer berries, and you have a winner!

The tanginess of the buttermilk balances the sweetness of the sugar and vanilla.

BUTTERMILK PUDDING INGREDIENTS

2 tablespoons water
¾ teaspoon unflavored gelatin
1 cup of heavy whipping cream
½ cup buttermilk
½ vanilla pod (split lengthwise)
¼ cup sugar
Pinch of fine sea salt

GARNISH INGREDIENTS

12 fresh raspberries
4 sprigs of mint

SUGAR SPUN BASKET

1½ cups of granulated sugar

RASPBERRY SAUCE INGREDIENTS

1 cup of raspberries
2 tablespoons of fine granulated sugar

CHOCOLATE SAUCE INGREDIENTS

1 cup of chocolate chips
¼ cup of whipping cream

HOW TO MAKE

1. Place 2 tablespoons of water into a small bowl and sprinkle over gelatin. Let it stand for 5 minutes until the gelatin softens.

2. In a saucepan, stir together the heavy cream, salt, and the sugar. Bring to a low boil and stir constantly for 3–5 minutes until the sugar has dissolved. Reduce the heat and stir in the gelatin mixture with the buttermilk, stirring until it has completely dissolved. Cook for 1 minute.

3. Strain the cream mixture through a sieve. Scrape the vanilla seeds from the pod and stir in at the end.

4. Divide into molds or ramekins. When cool they should be covered with plastic wrap and chilled for at least 4 hours in the refrigerator.

5. To make the sugar spun baskets, melt the sugar in a small skillet and boil until it is a light caramel color.

Remove from the heat and place the pan in a basin of cold water to stop the cooking process. Using the back of a spoon, drizzle the caramel in a thin steady stream moving back and forth to create a weave design. Gently remove each basket and place them on a sheet of parchment paper.

6. To make the sauces, purée the raspberries and sugar together and strain to remove the seeds. Melt the chocolate over a double boiler with the cream and stir to melt. Transfer to squeeze bottles.

7. To serve, remove the buttermilk pudding from the mold and place in the center of the plate. Place three raspberries on the side of the panna cotta and a sprig of mint. Using a squeeze bottle pour three circles of raspberry sauce and a swirl of chocolate sauce. Gently place the sugar spun basket on top

Dark Chocolate Ganache with Cashel Blue Cheese

This wonderful combination is a creation of my Irish celebrity chef friend, Noel McMeel. It is also special to me as it is one of the courses, we presented at our James Beard House Irish dinner in New York a few years back. The opportunity to cook at the James Beard House will remain one of the greatest honors of my life, and it was such a joy to showcase Irish food as being worthy of world class status.

The combination of chocolate and blue cheese here is surprising at first, but when combined with a dessert wine or port it becomes a taste bud sensation.

The Catalina Restaurant at the 5-star Lough Erne Resort in County Fermanagh, classifies this as a *prédessert,* so you could serve this at a party as your guests arrive. Feel free to substitute other blue cheeses, such as Roquefort, Stilton, or Gorgonzola, if Cashel Blue Irish Cheese is not available.

Enjoy!

GANACHE INGREDIENTS

1 cup heavy cream
12 ounces 60% bittersweet chocolate
8 ounces (1 cup) unsalted Irish butter (room temperature)
Pinch of Fleur de Sel (or other fine sea salt)

CASHEL BLUE CHEESE INGREDIENTS

1 ounce slice of Cashel Blue per person

HOW TO MAKE

1. Place the cream in a saucepan and bring to a low boil reducing until the quantity is 50 percent to thicken and allow the moisture to naturally evaporate.

2. Sir in the chocolate until it has melted. Whisk in the softened unsalted butter until smooth and glossy.

3. Transfer chocolate mixture to a shallow pan and refrigerate until firm.

4. Using the two tablespoons to form a quenelle. It is helpful to dip the two spoons in hot water that will help to release the quenelle. Pass the ganache repeatedly between the spoons, turning until the quenelle shape is formed. If you prefer you can also dip a spoon in hot water and create a chocolate curl.

5. The ganache is best stored and served from the refrigerator until ready to serve.

6. Slice Cashel blue cheese into neat triangles (all the same size).

7. To serve, place one triangle of blue cheese and one quenelle of ganache on each plate for pre-dessert.

From Green Fields to Kitchen Tables

Rustic Irish foods that warm the heart

The increasing popularity of farmers markets throughout Ireland is a clear sign of the demand for farm fresh produce. St. George's Market in Belfast and the English Market in Cork, to name just two, are busy every day with visitors and tourists browsing through the incredible products straight from the land and the sea. From seaweed to Irish breads, fish and meats of every sort, the simplicity and purity of Irish produce is the crowning glory of the land.

There is a new pride in the quality of the ingredients in an Irish meal. Where else has a climate so utterly suited to rearing world-class beef, lamb, and pork and to growing vegetables like the Comber Early potato and the soup celery only found in the north of Ireland? Each region has its specialties for sure, but the common thread is always the nutrient-rich grass which thrives in the rain. It is why Ireland has those Forty Shades of Green and it is also the foundation of so many delicious foods and drinks.

A glass of cold Irish milk with a slice of bread spread with golden butter is surely one of the best snacks in the world!

Leaving America

For Etta and John, returning to Ireland was not without regret and times of reflective sadness. I am sure it was bittersweet for them to think back on those formative days in America, with all their struggles and achievements.

Everyone who has experienced the pangs of immigration will know how the heart can be in two places at the same time, but in the end, it was the land that mended their souls and allowed them to settle back in those green fields of home again.

The fertile Irish soil grows the most wonderful vegetables with the damp climate lending itself to crops including potatoes, carrots,

A RETURN TO IRELAND

turnips, cabbages, and leeks. After returning to the land from urban Boston, I can only imagine the satisfaction of digging vegetables grown from seed, breaking off the stalk for mulch and walking with hands full to the kitchen. My own family also grew their own potatoes. Nothing beats the flavor of vegetables that have been freshly dug that day. The slow simmer in the farmhouse kitchen renders the white floury flesh that awaits the bouquet of spring onions that all Irish people adore.

Depending on the part of the country you are in, they call it colcannon, champ or cally. Indeed, ask some farmers today what their favorite dinner is, and they will say boiled potatoes with salt and pepper, sliced onion, and plenty of butter. It is a rare Irish person who likes waxy potatoes. The gold standard is the "balls of flour" moniker. Even potatoes which were past their best were not wasted. A border county specialty is boxty—not unlike a rosti. The potato is grated, and flour and seasoning added before it is fried in butter. Locals say it tastes better with potatoes they would describe as "soapy". The legacy of the Potato Famine lingers long.

John and Etta's farm in the shadow of the Mourne mountains was small by today's standards, but they both learned to expertly work the land and provide for their family. They tilled the soil to bring small crops to turn a profit, and in time added a few cattle to the holdings. I always was amazed at the gardening skills of my grandfather who managed a walled kitchen garden during my childhood, and he seemed to be able to grow anything. Skills learned from his parents no doubt as the produce on the table depended on the growth from the soil. No doubt he was taught how to "chit" potatoes so that they would sprout roots. They would then be planted for the next crop. A different perspective on food from those days that I am passionate about rekindling today.

Food From the Field

A sense of place has always been important in Irish culture, and food has now found its identity in this new era with Irish chefs and cooks honoring the produce that makes Irish cuisine so exciting. Think of the County Fermanagh butcher Pat O'Doherty, has dedicated a whole island for his pigs to run around which he calls 'Inish Corkish', to produce the most delicious nitrate free Fermanagh Black Bacon. Richard and Leona Kane's Broighter Gold farm in County Derry is famous for its golden fields of rapeseed in the springtime. They have become a tourist attraction as they highlight the landscape. The oils are Ireland's version of olive oil and are infused with many flavors such as hickory smoke.

Chefs have discovered the very elements that make Ireland so great, her rich produce, hidden for so many years by poverty and exploitation. They are proud to proclaim their presence on their menus. In fact, when visiting Ireland for the first time many of my tour guests break all their dietary rules surrounded by the abundance of wonderful foods from the land. Take for example the famous hearty Irish breakfast, enjoyed by most visitors to the island, with its local sausages, hearty bacon, mushrooms, tomatoes, potato farls, soda bread, black pudding and eggs with bright yellow yolks. One breakfast is almost enough for the entire day!

It is tradition to have copious cups of tea throughout the day. You could have "a cup in your hand" but no-one ever refuses a slice of apple tart or a traybake. The home-baking tradition ranges from the Ulster soda farls to the Tipperary Grinder and the brown wheaten bread to the sweet treats of Fifteens and shortbreads.

Ireland has been born again with food from the field in abundance and becoming famous throughout Europe as her producers export their world-class meat, vegetables, milk, cheese, butter, breads, beers, ciders and condiments. So, join me on a journey into some of my favorite rustic Irish dishes the Etta would have been proud of.

CHAPTER SIX

Rustic Ireland

Wexford Strawberry Salad with Mint Tea Vinaigrette
(page 159)

Bircher Overnight Oats with Macerated Berries

Serves 4–6

The Irish have been eating oats for centuries, long before it was ever trending and a known super food. Our farmhouse kitchen always had a pot of what we called "porridge" on the go in the morning, and most Irish started their day this way.

Many of the hoteliers we work with in Ireland offer an Irish Style *Bircher Oatmeal* and soak their oats in part apple juice, which is a wonderful and flavorful way to kick start your day. This allows for speedy breakfast on-the-go. Just grab a spoon and dig right in!

OATS INGREDIENTS

2 cups jumbo old fashioned rolled oats
2–3 tablespoons mixed seeds (chia, pumpkin, sunflower, flax)
1¾ cups of milk (you can use dairy or dairy free almond, oat, or coconut milk)
¼ cup of apple juice
2 tablespoons lemon juice

IN THE MORNING INGREDIENTS

1 apple (cored and grated with skin on)
1 cup of whole milk yogurt
1 tablespoon raw honey
1 teaspoon bourbon vanilla
Pinch of salt

MACERATED BERRIES INGREDIENTS

2 cups of berries (raspberries, blueberries, strawberries)
2 tablespoons of maple syrup
1 lemon (squeezed and zested)

HOW TO MAKE

1. To make the overnight oats, combine the oats and seeds with the milk, apple juice and lemon juice. Cover and soak for 6–8 hours or overnight in the refrigerator.

2. In the morning add the grated apple, honey and yogurt and stir to combine.

3. If using strawberries, remove the hard-central core at the stem with a paring knife. Slice the strawberries and toss them with blueberries and raspberries in the lemon juice and maple syrup.

4. To serve, divide overnight oats into bowls and spoon the macerated berries on top.

Red Velvet Beet Bowls with an Oaty Crunch

The beautiful red velvet bowl packs a nutritional punch along with the crunchy oat topping. Many of the castles, hotels and spas in Ireland today offer healthy options to pamper your body and soul, with so many wanting healthier and gluten and dairy free options, and the use of beets to get that vibrant color and taste is something you will see more and more of.

Beets are sweet and earthy and often overlooked as an interesting ingredient. They offer a welcome and colorful surprise in this cleansing and vibrant breakfast smoothie bowl.

SMOOTHIE BOWL INGREDIENTS

1 small beet (½ cup chopped roasted beets)
1 cup frozen raspberries 1 medium frozen banana
  (cut into pieces)
2 pitted dates
½ cup almond milk
¼ cup thick style whole milk yogurt (dairy free
  works too)

PEANUT OAT TOPPING INGREDIENTS

2 cups of old-fashioned oats
6 tablespoons of peanut butter
¼ teaspoon nutmeg
½ teaspoon cinnamon
¼ cup of honey
1 teaspoon of vanilla
Pinch of kosher salt

HOW TO MAKE

1. Preheat oven to 375°F. Wrap the beet in foil and bake for about an hour or until it has softened. Remove from the oven and allow cooling.

2. Place the beets, berries, banana, pitted dates, almond milk and Yogurt in a blender and blend until it has a smooth consistency. Refrigerate until ready to use.

3. To make the peanut butter granola preheat the oven to 325°F.

4. In a medium size bowl, mix together the oats, salt and cinnamon and nutmeg. In a small saucepan melt the peanut butter, honey, and vanilla together and whisk until they are smooth. Pour over the oats and toss until they are well combined.

5. Grease a cookie sheet and bake the oat mixture for 18–22 minutes stirring halfway through to ensure an even crunchy golden-brown granola. Allow the granola to cool and harden.

6. To serve, fill a small bowl with the beet berry purée and top with a breakup the peanut butter granola and sprinkle over the smoothie bowl.

Irish Cured Ham
& Cheddar Cheese Pillows

ᕽ   *Serves 4–6*   ᕻ

When you visit Ireland, it is not unusual for some eateries to have their own hens laying fresh eggs on the property as well as having their own garden for fresh herbs and vegetables. It is a return to the kitchen gardens of old, especially in some of the older houses and castles such as Killeavy Castle in County Down and Ballynahinch in Connemara.

Smaller flocks of hens are happier when there is no competition for food or pasture, and amusing as this sounds, the happiness is transferred to the taste of the eggs!

I serve these Irish cured ham cheddar cheese pillows for brunch events, and they are always especially appreciated by those looking for a wonderful gluten free alternative. These colorful pillowy bites melt in your mouth when pulled straight from the oven.

INGREDIENTS FOR PILLOWS

1 teaspoon of canola oil and a standard size muffin tin
12 slices cured ham of prosciutto ham
3 medium size eggs (beaten)
4 fluid ounces (½ cup) heavy cream
2 ounces (½ cup) mature cheddar cheese
Sea salt and freshly milled black pepper
Small handful of spinach leaves (torn)

INGREDIENTS TO FINISH

4 basil leaves (torn)
6 cherry tomatoes (cut in half)

HOW TO MAKE

1. Preheat the oven to 350°F.

2. Lightly grease a standard size muffin tin with canola oil.

3. Line each muffin tin indentation with a slice of prosciutto to create a base.

4. Whisk the eggs, cream, cheese, spinach, and season with salt and pepper in a bowl. Transfer the mixture to a pouring jug and divide between the muffin cups.

5. Place half a tomato in the center of each cup and a little torn basil.

6. Bake in the oven for 12–15 minutes or until the egg mixture has almost set (the egg should jiggle slightly when you shake the muffin pan, and the center should test clean when inserted.

7. Best served warm straight from the oven.

Wexford Strawberry Salad with Mint Tea Vinaigrette

Serves 4–6

The warmer climate and the quality of the soils in County Wexford have made the area famous for some of the most flavorsome strawberries on the island. It is called the Sunny Southeast. When in Ireland, the best strawberries can be purchased on the side of the road by local growers selling freshly picked fruits from the field.

The strawberry skins are so tender, and the fruit is so red to the very core, a true taste of an Irish summer.

SPINACH SALAD INGREDIENTS

6 cups of baby spinach
1 pound strawberries (hulled and sliced)
2 small avocados (peeled, pitted and diced)
4 ounces blue cheese (Cashel Blue or Stilton)
⅓ cup blanched whole almonds (toasted and chopped)
Sea salt

MINT TEA VINAIGRETTE

¼ cup balsamic vinegar
1 mint tea bag
1 tablespoon shallot (very finely chopped)
2 tablespoons wild honey
½ cup olive oil
Sea salt and freshly ground black pepper
Small handful of basil leaves (chopped)

HOW TO MAKE

1. To make the vinaigrette, heat the balsamic vinegar in a small saucepan to simmering and then add the mint tea bag to infuse for 3 minutes. Remove tea bag and add the raw honey, salt, and pepper to vinegar mixture. Whisk in the olive oil and fresh basil.

2. Add the spinach greens on individual plates or place in a large salad bowl. Season greens with a little salt and freshly ground black pepper.

3. Preheat the oven to 350°F. Place the almonds on a baking tray and toast for 6–7 minutes until they are golden and fragrant.

4. Prepare the avocado, cut each one in half and remove the stone. Use a knife to slice the inside of the avocado into sections and use your fingers to separate the avocado segments from the peel.

5. To assemble the salad, place the greens in a bowl and then add the strawberries, avocado, blue cheese, and almonds.

6. Toss with the vinaigrette just before serving.

Golden Barley & Garden Pea Summer Salad

Serves 4

Golden Barley has been waving in the Irish wind for centuries, used for distilling and in all of our delicious soups and stews. Ancient grains, including barley, are making a comeback because the food industry realizes the value of good nutrition. Pearly barley contains more vitamins, minerals and fiber than found in modern grains, and it has a lovely mild nutty flavor, and a chewy texture.

In our Irish farmhouse garden, we always grew garden peas that were so sweet and tender in the summer months. I was often given the tedious job of shelling a bucket of peas from their pods as a child, and I remember eating as many of them as I could while shelling. For fun, I have also added some sweet corn, fresh herbs, and suggest a mild sheep's cheese to pair well with this delightful salad!

BARLEY SALAD INGREDIENTS

2 cups pearl barley (cooked)
½ cup fresh summer peas (blanched)
1 ear of corn (½ cup) fresh summer corn kernels (grilled
4 ounces local semi soft sheep milk cheese (crumbled by hand)

VINAIGRETTE INGREDIENTS

1 tablespoon lemon juice
1 clove of garlic (crushed)
1 teaspoon maple syrup
3 tablespoons olive oil
Flakey sea salt and freshly ground black pepper
Kosher salt and freshly ground black pepper

GARNISH INGREDIENTS

4 tablespoons garden herbs (mint, Italian parsley, chives)
Handful of pea shoots

HOW TO MAKE

1. Cook the pearl barley in plenty of water and salt. Drain and set aside to cool.

2. Grill the corn and allow it to blacken a little. Allow the corn to cool, and then use a knife to remove the kernels.

3. Cook the peas until they are tender crisp (they should only take 3–4 minutes when they are cooked in boiling salted water). When they are cooked, strain the peas over cold running water or plunge them into an ice bath, so they do not continue to cook.

4. To make the vinaigrette, whisk the lemon juice, garlic, maple syrup together and then the olive oil at the end. Season with salt and pepper.

5. Toss the barley, corn and peas in the vinaigrette and place on a platter. Sprinkle over the cheese and finally the garden herbs and pea shoots.

Crispy Kale Salad with Baked Irish Cheese & a Lemon Vinaigrette

Kale has become a popular superfood in dishes crafted all over the world, and the Irish love it too. Kale favors the Irish climate and grows throughout the island. It is packed with natural green chlorophyll and makes the perfect base for nutrient dense salads.

The beauty of this salad is that not only is it perfect for entertaining; it is also unique in that the flavor of the kale is improved by marinating, so we suggest adding the vinaigrette up to an hour before serving.

This kale salad was crafted to share on my cooking school tours, and it was also used when I was featured on NPR sharing a special menu for families to enjoy for St. Patrick's Day. We hope you enjoy it, too!

SALAD INGREDIENTS

1 bunch of kale (rough stems removed)
1 carrot (ribboned)
½ cup of red cabbage (finely chopped)
¼ cup spring onions (chopped)
2 tablespoons sunflower seeds (roasted and salted)

CRISPY BAKED CHEESE INGREDIENTS

½ cup Parmesan Reggiano or Dubliner cheddar Irish cheese (freshly grated)

VINAIGRETTE INGREDIENTS

1½ tablespoons of lemon juice
1 teaspoon lemon zest
1½ teaspoons whole grain mustard
1 teaspoon raw honey
¼ teaspoon of kosher salt
3 tablespoons olive oil
Freshly milled black pepper

HOW TO MAKE

1. To make the vinaigrette, whisk together the lemon juice, lemon zest, mustard, honey and salt and pepper in a large salad bowl. Slowly whisk in the olive oil until fully incorporated.

2. Add the kale to the vinaigrette and red cabbage and toss, allowing it to marinade and soften in the refrigerator for 30 minutes to an hour.

3. To make the crispy baked cheese, preheat the oven to 400°F and line a baking tray with parchment paper.

Sprinkle the cheese over the baking sheet in a thin layer. Bake in the oven for 7 minutes or until the cheese is golden brown and lacy. Wait for a few minutes until the cheese is hard and crispy and then break it up with hands or cut with a sharp knife to make the cheese crisps.

4. To serve the salad, divide the kale on to plates and then top with the prepared carrot, spring onion and sunflower seeds. Finish the dish by adding three pieces of the crispy baked cheese on each plate.

Baby Potato Salad with a Garden Herb Mayo

When you travel to Ireland you will finally get to taste the goodness of flavorful Irish Potatoes. The Irish climate and soil are the perfect conditions for growing those delicious balls of white floury potatoes, or *spuds* as we like to call them in Ireland!

Potato Salad is such a popular side dish, and we add some spring onions or scallions along with lots of fresh fragrant garden herbs.

Fingerling potatoes offer a variety of shapes, and they make a lovely presentation, although baby potatoes will also be delicious for this recipe.

POTATO SALAD INGREDIENTS

1 pound fingerling potatoes or baby potatoes
2 tablespoons apple cider vinegar

DRESSING INGREDIENTS

4 tablespoons mayonnaise
4 tablespoons natural yogurt
1 teaspoon Dijon mustard
1 teaspoon smoked paprika

GREENS INGREDIENTS

8 spring onions (green parts only)
3 tablespoons garden herbs (mint, tarragon, chives, or dill) (chopped)
Sea salt and freshly ground pepper

GARNISH

3 slices bacon (cooked crispy and chopped)

HOW TO MAKE

1. Bring a large pot of salted water to a boil.
2. While waiting for water to boil, cook the bacon in a pan or bake in the oven until crispy and set aside.
3. Add the fingerling potatoes to the pot and once the water has returned to the boil lower the heat and cook the potatoes for 10–12 minutes or until they are tender when pierced with a fork.
4. Drain the potatoes and toss in apple cider vinegar. To make the dressing combine the mayonnaise, yogurt, mustard, paprika, salt and freshly ground pepper.
5. Gently combine the dressing, herbs, spring onions and potatoes and transfer to a serving bowl.
6. Chop the bacon finely and sprinkle over the potatoes for a garnish.
7. Chill in the refrigerator until ready to serve.

Citrus & Herb Roasted Goose

Serves 4–6

Game hunting is a popular pastime in rural Ireland where farmers often shoot goose, duck, pheasant, and other fowl for the purpose of the sport and for food on the table.

In the farming community, around the Christmas season, there is a culture of giving gifts from the farm to neighbors and friends. Each year my family would receive a glorious, fattened goose from our neighbor, which would herald in the much-anticipated feast to come. The meat is moist and flavorful and a wonderful roast to enjoy anytime of the year, or as a special holiday celebration.

Do not forget to keep the fat to rub on your leather shoes to keep them in good condition. If you are lucky enough to get a goose with feathers on, keep the wing as a feather duster. Waste not, want not.

GOOSE INGREDIENTS

10 pound oven-ready goose at room temperature
1 tablespoon olive oil
2 tablespoons of honey
2 teaspoons thyme leaves

DRY CITRUS RUB INGREDIENTS

1 orange zested
1 lemon (zested)
1 tablespoon light brown sugar
1 tablespoon Chinese five spice (mix of cinnamon, clove, fennel seed, star anise and Sichuan peppercorn)
1 teaspoon kosher salt
¼ teaspoon garlic powder
½ teaspoons cayenne pepper
½ teaspoons ground black pepper

JUS FINISHING INGREDIENTS

2 tablespoons sherry vinegar
Splash of water

HOW TO MAKE

1. Preheat the oven to 400°F.
2. To make the citrus rub, zest the oranges and lemons and combine all the dry ingredients.
3. To prepare the goose, score the skin in a crisscross fashion to help the fat render when roasting in the oven. Begin to rub the citrus rub both inside and outside of the bird. Slice the zested oranges in half and stuff them inside of the goose with the lemons. Tuck the neck flap under the goose and then lift the legs and wings to help them brown better.
4. Drizzle the goose with a little olive oil for a crispy skin followed by the honey and sprinkle over the thyme leaves evenly over the skin.
5. Place the goose in a large heavy based roasting tin and put in the prepared oven. Roast the goose at a higher heat for the first hour and then reduce the oven temperature down to 350°F for the remaining time. Allow 15 minutes per pound so the total amount of cooking time should be 3 hours. During the cooking time drain off any excess fat and base the goose with the pan juices (this should be done every 30 minutes or so because there will be a lot of rendered fat during roasting).
6. Remove the goose from the oven and allow it to rest for 30 minutes loosely covered with aluminum foil.
7. Drain off any remaining fat and reserve it all for another purpose (roasting potatoes or vegetables). Place goose on a carving board and slice for serving. Add the sherry vinegar and a splash of water to the sticky pan juices and drizzle over the carved goose.

Crispy Goose Fat Roasted Potatoes

Serves 4–6

Almost as important as the roasted meat, are the roasted potatoes! Achieving the perfect crispiness on the outside, combined with a fluffy floury potato inside is to me an art form. My grandmother seemed to effortlessly achieve the most incredible roast potatoes and our family secret has always been to use the fat from the goose combined with semolina flour for the crispiness on the outside.

We taste-tested this recipe with Yukon Gold potatoes that have an ideal texture that hold together when roasting.

CRISPY POTATO INGREDIENTS

2 pounds Yukon Golds or King Edward potatoes (peeled)
2 tablespoons semolina flour
3–4 tablespoons of goose fat (unsalted butter can be substituted)
Sea salt and freshly ground black pepper
3 sprigs of thyme (leaves picked and finely chopped)
Flakey salt (to finish)

HOW TO MAKE

1. Preheat the oven to 450°F.

2. Spoon the duck fat into a roasting tin and set in the oven so it gets extremely hot (this should take about 20 minutes).

3. Cut the potatoes so they are even in size slicing them in quarters or thirds depending on the size of your potatoes. Place the potatoes in a medium size saucepan of cold salted water, bring them to a boil and cook for about 5 minutes.

4. Drain the potatoes and then transfer them back to the dry saucepan. Sprinkle over the semolina flour and gently shake the saucepan so that the potatoes are coated, and the potatoes are a little ruffled (this will help them become extra crunchy later).

5. Transfer the potatoes into the roasting pan with the hot duck fat and half of the chopped thyme tossing to coat them evenly. Roast the potatoes for about 45 minutes turning them over to brown evenly after the first 25 minutes of cooking.

6. When the potatoes are crispy and roasted transfer them to a warmed serving plate. Sprinkle over the remaining chopped thyme. Sprinkle with a little flakey sea salt to finish.

Atlantic Cod in a Green Jacket with Herb Butter

Serves 4

Unlike the traditional white cabbage that we are all familiar with, the savoy cabbage is a bright green in color, with a curly ruffled textured leaf. When steamed, it holds it vibrancy and it is pleasantly soft with a delicate flavor. The leaves are also ideal for sautéing because it is not naturally crispy. In this dish, the balance of flavor works really well with a flaky white fish such as Atlantic cod.

Any good white flakey fish will work with this dish, such as cod, plaice or halibut, but my preference is cod. Caught in the cold Atlantic waters and loved by the Irish.

COD INGREDIENTS

4 medium savoy cabbage leaves (large vein removed)
4 (6–8 ounces) cod white fish fillets
Sea salt and pepper
Water (to poach the fish)

HERB BUTTER SAUCE INGREDIENTS

½ cup dry white wine
¼ cup lemon juice
3 tablespoons shallots (finely chopped)
1 tablespoon crème fraiche
8 tablespoons unsalted room temperature butter
  (cut into small pieces)
½ teaspoon kosher salt
½ teaspoon black pepper
2 tablespoons chives (chopped)
2 tablespoons parsley (chopped)

HOW TO MAKE

1. Preheat the oven to 350°F.

2. Bring a large pot of salted water to a boil and blanch the savoy cabbage leaves for just a few seconds and then refresh in a bowl of ice water.

3. In a large, buttered dish lay out the blanched leaves and place a piece of fish on one end of each leaf. Season the fish on both sides with a little salt and fresh ground black pepper. Fold the other side of the cabbage leaf over and tuck in to make a little green jacket. Trim with a knife if necessary.

4. Pour a little water over the fillets and cover with buttered parchment paper and steam in oven for 10–12 minutes, until the fish is white and flakey.

5. To make the sauce reduce the white wine with the lemon juice and shallots, gently simmering for 5 minutes or until the liquid is reduced by half. Whisk in the crème fraiche and continue to simmer for 1 more minute. Remove the pan from the heat and whisk in the butter, one piece at a time. Stir in the chives and parsley. Season the sauce with a little salt and pepper.

6. To serve, place the fish on a plate and drizzle with a little of the sauce. Serve immediately and enjoy!

Meringue Nests with Vanilla Cream & a Ginger Peach Topping

These delicate and petite crunchy bites are very elegant, especially for a spring tea event, and make interesting additions to any table. Differing flavors and colors can be added to these little delights, with some other suggested toppings being strawberries and rose scented cream or mint essence cream and dark chocolate.

Once you have mastered the basic meringue recipe, though, you can add your own flavor and twist as you desire. In this version, I have honored my Georgia surroundings and plumbed for peaches on top!

MERINGUE INGREDIENTS

2 large egg whites (room temperature)
¼ teaspoon cream of tartar or white wine vinegar
½ teaspoon pure vanilla extract
½ cup plus 1 tablespoon fine granulated sugar
Pinch of salt

PEACH CREAM INGREDIENTS

¼ cup heavy whipping cream
2 teaspoons sugar
1 teaspoon vanilla
1 teaspoon fresh ginger juice
5 fresh peaches (peeled and chopped) or preserved peaches
6 mint leaves (chiffonade cut)

HOW TO MAKE

1. Preheat your oven to 200°F, then line a large baking tray with wax paper.

2. Beat the egg whites, and salt at medium low speed in an electric mixer until stiff and foamy (but not dry).

3. Add the cream of tartar and the sugar 1 teaspoon at a time, increasing the speed to a medium-high until fully incorporated.

4. Transfer the meringue mixture into a piping bag with a ½-inch 6-point star nozzle and pipe round circles onto the lined baking tray in the shape of a bird's nest (I do this by piping a round circle base and then without lifting the piping bag piping circles around the edge of the circle base).

5. Bake the meringues in the oven for 1 hour until the meringues are dry. Switch off the oven and leave them to crisp with oven door slightly open for one to two hours or until they have cooled. (I like to leave them overnight with the oven light on to further dry them out).

6. To make the filling, beat the heavy whipping cream, vanilla, and sugar until stiff.

7. Decorate by filling the ½-inch 6-star nozzle with fresh cream and pipe to fill each nest center (toss the peaches in the fresh ginger juice). Top with the diced peaches and garnish with a chiffonade cut mint.

Petit Fours:
White Chocolate & Coconut Fifteens

Fifteens are one of Northern Ireland's most famous teatime treat, and it was the first thing that I ever made in the kitchen by myself as young girl. Over the years I have tweaked the recipe a little, and I love to replace the traditional glaze cherries with white chocolate chips, dried cranberries, or pistachios.

Define a fifteen? Simply speaking, the name derives from the fact that we use a quantity of fifteen for each ingredient used. There, mystery solved!

FIFTEENS INGREDIENTS

15 digestive biscuits (or substitute with 8 graham crackers)
15 large multicolored marshmallows (snip with scissors or ¼ cup of mini marshmallows)
15 squares of white chocolate chopped (or 200 g of white chocolate chips)
1 cup (200 ml) sweetened condensed milk
1 tablespoon water
Unsweetened fine coconut (for rolling)

HOW TO MAKE

1. In a food processor, crush the digestive biscuits or graham crackers.

2. In a large bowl, mix the crushed biscuits, chopped marshmallows, white chocolate and cherries and the sweetened condensed milk and water.

3. Lay out a large sheet of parchment or plastic wrap and sprinkle with coconut. Spread the prepared mixture along the plastic wrap to form a long sausage shape. Sprinkle more coconut over the top of the mixture and then begin to roll using the parchment paper to form a circular sausage shape. Twist both ends to seal.

4. Refrigerate for at least 4 hours or allow to sit overnight before slicing into 15 pieces (naturally)!

A RETURN TO IRELAND

Petit Fours:
Coconut Oat Truffles

Makes 2–2½ dozen

These wonderful little Coconut Oat Truffles provide a healthy gluten-free option when serving petit fours.

COCONUT OAT TRUFFLE INGREDIENTS

2¼ unsweetened cups coconut
2 cups gluten free rolled oats (lightly toasted)
¾ cup mini dark chocolate chips
1 cup nut butter (almond, cashew, or peanut)
¼ raw honey
1 teaspoon vanilla and a pinch of sea salt

HOW TO MAKE

1. Lightly process 2 cups of the coconut with the toasted oats in a processor for a few seconds. Add the nut butter, honey, chocolate chips, vanilla and salt and pulse to combine everything.

2. Roll into balls and toss in the reserved ¼ cup of coconut. Add 1–2 tablespoons of honey if the mixture is too dry to form balls.

Feasts, Friendship & Folklore

Foods of Irish legends and folklore

Ancient beliefs and legends have been part of the fabric of life in Ireland for thousands of years. Stories have been passed down from generation to generation, such as with the legend of St. Brigid whose feast honors the Celtic first day of Spring, February 1st. They say her beauty was such that she stopped traffic in Dundalk so she plucked out her eye to avoid vanity. There is an eye-shaped stone in her shrine at Faughart in memory of this. St Patrick was actually a Welsh slave who drove the snakes out of Ireland. Walk his trail in Downpatrick in County Down.

Irish people give thanks for the bounty of the land on this day, pray for protection and look forward to the lengthening of days as they make crosses from reeds to hang on their doorways. In ancient times, this was what was known the feast of *Imbolc*. It is considered bad luck to put out the ashes on May Day and no-one ever cuts down a tree which grows in the middle of a field for fear of angering the fairies who live there. You will often see them left alone in farms all over the country.

The months of January to March were called the "Hungry Gap" because all that was in season were cabbage and turnips. Today of course we have the benefit of grocery stores with a wide variety of produce available all year around, but none the less, it is good to pause and consider where our food comes from and find some way to honor the miracle of food through feast and folklore.

Continuing Culture

John and Etta built their life as Irish farmers on the land they inherited, and the generations that came after them, including myself, benefited from that wealth of Irish culture with all of its traditions and legends. Isn't it true that we all take our inherited culture for granted? Until the moment arrives when we leave the land of our birth, only then do we discover that our beliefs, our community, and the folklore of our place are somewhat unique. John and Etta knew this from their immigrant adventures, the struggles they faced in a new land, and 100 years later, I too understand just what it means to leave your home-place, with all its friendship and folklore, and carve out a new life in a new land.

As an Irish immigrant, my food heritage is important to my sense of place. My being able to share these stories with my new friends in my adopted home became a lifeline. Just like many immigrants before me, I went through the ebb and flow of culture shock. I experienced good days

when I felt alive and free in my new world, and bad days, when my heart felt sick, and I longed for Ireland. Cooking Irish food with all of its traditional memories became the magical glue that solidified that pang for home in my heart and has acted like a healing medicine for the soul. It is a deep well from which I draw strength and sustenance.

And so it is that some of the recipes in this chapter are inspired by Irish legends, whilst others are legendary through Irish tradition and regional to the area, I grew up in. Yes, food can be culture.

I would not consider my own father to be romantic, but every year at springtime he would ceremoniously pick the first primroses when they appeared on his farmland, and hand them to my mother. That bunch of flowers heralded the beginning of spring for our family, as a sign of milder weather. My dad was a sheep farmer, so for him it was a time to reflect on the upcoming lambing season and the end of winter. Before long, we would be sniffing the honeyed and coconut-like scents from the yellow gorse and hawthorn, knowing that longer days were ahead.

My birthday falls on the summer solstice, June 21st. It has been a feast day of significance in Ireland for millennia where we celebrate the rising of the mid-summer sun. People gather at the ancient site of Newgrange in Meath to see the sun rise at dawn when the light comes through the corbelled roof at this passage grave, Ireland's Stonehenge.

The smell of fresh cut grass is everywhere signaling a busy time on the farm when the silage is to be cut and stored to feed cattle in the bleak winter. The wild Irish rose, and the honeysuckle are in full bloom in the hedgerows. Their heady floral scent fills the air. The elder is growing wild throughout the island, and both the elderflower and the

elderberry are widely used to garnish salads, as a flavoring to puddings, syrup, and gin. Elderflower cordial and elderberry jelly infused with port are two popular recipes among the growing number of foragers. It is a time of plenty.

Then, as the shadows start to lengthen, we celebrate Halloween on October 31st each year. Originating in Ireland from the Celtic festival called "Samhain", which signifies the end of summer, there are many legendary food traditions throughout Ireland for this feast, include eating Colcannon, or baking barmbrack with dried summer fruits and spices. A gold ring is hidden inside wrapped in greaseproof paper to bring luck to the recipient. In County Armagh, the orchard county of Ireland, my Halloween food memories recall the abundance of apples. We would drink apple cider, eat toffee apples and caramel apples, apple pies, cakes, fritters, creams, and dumplings, and play a game ducking our heads into a basin of water to catch an apple with our teeth. No pumpkins, but turnips instead and a season of rich heritage.

And finally, as the year concludes, the winter solstice on December 21st comes upon us as the shortest day of the year. It too is an ancient Celtic festival, marked with feasting, dancing and the celebration of the goodness of the earth. Many of the foods we associate in Ireland with Christmas, have roots with the older winter solstice legends. The spices added to winter fruits and the aromas wafting through the home are that nod to the harvest end, preservation, rebirth, and renewal. The family gather around the table to share plum pudding, fruit cakes, mince pies and the festive spiced beef which originated in Cork, as the earth prepares to usher in another new year.

So, join me as we celebrate the feast and festival food of Ireland with all of its rich traditions.

CHAPTER SEVEN

Legendary
Ireland Dishes

Colcannon Potatoes
(page 195)

Dingle Town Puck Pie

෨   *Makes 6 larger pies or 12 small pies*   ෮

Regional fairs are held all over Ireland. They started as a gathering place to sell cattle and horses and over the years have developed into community and cultural events with some incredible food.

In August, the Lamas Day holiday is closely tied to the ancient Celtic festival of Lughnasagh and in the Kingdom of Kerry, in Dingle Town, lamb pies are sold at the Puck Fair each year. These tasty individual pies are easy to carry around and they would be traditionally sold from a stall at the fair.

Try accompanying Dingle Pies with Tzatziki sauce (yogurt, cucumber, dill, and garlic)!

LAMB FILLING INGREDIENTS

1 pound lamb shoulder (cut in to 1-inch cubes)
2 tablespoons olive oil
1 small onion, chopped
1 small carrot finely chopped
1 bay leaf
2 tablespoons flour (blended in ¼ cup water)
3½ cups beef or lamb stock
1 tablespoon fresh mint (chopped)
Sea salt and white pepper
Sprig of rosemary (leaves picked)

PASTRY INGREDIENTS

2 cups all-purpose flour
1 tablespoon fine granulated sugar
1 teaspoon salt
¾ cups unsalted butter
1 egg beaten with 1 tablespoon milk
1 egg mixed with 1 tablespoon water
Pinch of fine sea salt

HOW TO MAKE

1. Season the lamb with salt and pepper.

2. Preheat a large cast iron saucepan to medium high heat with the oil and butter combined.

3. Add the lamb to skillet and cook the cubes in small batches for 2–3 minutes on each side to brown and sear. Add all the lamb back to the saucepan and then add the onions and cook for another 5 minutes, stirring occasionally. Preheat the oven to 325°F.

4. Combine the stock, flour, and pour over the casserole. Add the carrot, fresh rosemary, and the bay leaf. Cover and cook low and slow in the oven for 1 hour, until the lamb is tender and falling apart. Remove the bay leaf and cool. Stir in the fresh chopped mint.

5. To make the pastry, measure the flour, sugar, and salt together and rub in the butter using your hands until it resembles coarse meal. Use a knife to stir in the beaten egg and milk until the pastry comes together (adding a little extra milk if needed).

6. Divide the pastry in to 6 equal portions and roll into individual balls. Wrap up the pastry and chill for at least 1 hour. Using a rolling pin and extra flour, make even discs. Spoon the meat mixture over one half of each pastry circle. Wet the edges with egg washing using a pastry brush. Fold over and press down with a fork or using your thumb to press down to create an edge. Brush the pies all over the top with wash.

7. Bake the pies for 15–18 minutes until they are golden brown.

Wandering Aengus Trout

Serves 4

Trout stories and legends are common all over Ireland, with many summer ponds, lakes, streams, and holy wells being haunted by the "blessed fish." In the West of Ireland, the legend of the "White Trout of Cong" is an ancient magical folklore tale of romance and tragedy. William Butler Yeats included the tale in collection "Fairy Folk Tales of the Irish Peasantry," in 1888.

Trout has a delicate flavor, which loves soft herbs like basil and the sweet beetroot.

TROUT INGREDIENTS

4 (4-ounce) rainbow trout fillets (scaled)
1 tablespoon vegetable oil
1 tablespoon salted butter
1 teaspoon sea salt
1 teaspoon freshly ground black pepper
2 radishes (finely sliced)

BEETROOT PURÉE INGREDIENTS

3 small size beets
4 tablespoons red wine vinegar
3–5 tablespoons water (to make a smooth sauce)
Salt and freshly ground black pepper

FOR THE BASIL PURÉE

3 ounces basil leaves
2 ounces baby spinach leaves
2 ounces olive oil
4 ounces water (reserved)
Salt and freshly ground black pepper

OAT CRUMBLE INGREDIENTS

¼ cup jumbo oats
1½ tablespoons butter
Pinch salt

184   A RETURN TO IRELAND

HOW TO MAKE

1. To make the beetroot purée, preheat oven to 350°F. Wrap the beets in aluminum foil and bake in the oven for 1½ hours until they are tender. Allow to cool. Place the vinegar in a small saucepan and gently boil until it has reduced by half. Peel and chop the beets and then blend with the reduced vinegar, water, sea salt and freshly ground black pepper. Transfer to a squeeze bottle for plating.

2. To make the basil purée, bring water to boil in a medium saucepan and blanch the basil and spinach for one minute and then strain reserving 8 ounces of water. Blend the blanched basil, spinach and reserved water together. Season with salt and pepper and transfer into a squeeze bottle for plating.

3. To make the oat crumble, melt the butter on low and then add the oats stirring until they are browned and toasted. Remove from the heat and season with a little sea salt.

4. To prepare the trout, pat each fillet dry and then season with sea salt and pepper. Heat skillet to high and add vegetable oil and butter to a pan. Once the butter starts to foam, carefully add the trout fillets with the skin side down. Shake the pan to make sure the fish does not stick. Cook for about 2–3 minutes until the skin is a golden color and then turn over and cook for 2 more minutes on the other side.

5. To plate, serve the trout skin side up in the center of the plate. Spoon some of the basil purée on the side, beetroot purée, radish, and oat crumble.

The Salmon of Knowledge

Native Irish salmon, known as *Bradan* in Gaelic, are fished in the Atlantic Ocean and in the clear Irish rivers draining into it. Most rivers in Ireland also get a run of salmon from spring until autumn, and you can often see them leaping up in the water on their way to the mighty sea.

The Legend of the Salmon of Knowledge tells a story how Fionn Mac Cumhaill, became the great leader of the Fianna in Ireland. As a young man, he was a servant to a wise poet named Finnegas. The Story says that Finnegas caught a salmon and gave it to his servant instructing him not to eat it, because he knew they held special powers. The salmon had eaten nine hazelnuts that had fallen to the bottom of the well of wisdom from the nine trees growing around the well. As fate would have it, when Fionn was cooking the salmon, he accidently burnt his finger. Quickly, he put his finger in his mouth and he gained all the wisdom and knowledge in the world.

SALMON INGREDIENTS

4 (4-ounce) salmon fillets
Kosher salt and pepper to season
½ cup walnuts
½ cup old-fashioned oats
1 tablespoon sesame seeds
2 tablespoons dill (stalks removed)
1 tablespoon parsley
2 tablespoons Dijon mustard
2 tablespoons olive oil

GARDEN SALAD INGREDIENTS

4 handfuls of mixed greens
1 cup cherry tomatoes (cut in half horizontally)
Small handful of fresh herbs (parsley, dill)
2 green onions (finely chopped)

CARROT VINAIGRETTE INGREDIENTS

1 carrot, grated
1 tablespoon fresh minced ginger
2 tablespoons apple cider vinegar
1 teaspoon honey
2 tablespoons vegetable oil
1½ tablespoons miso
1 tablespoon water
1 tablespoon dark sesame oil
Kosher salt and pepper

HOW TO MAKE

1. Preheat the oven to 400°F.

2. In a food processor, combine the walnuts, oats, lemon zest and pulse. Add the dill and parsley and pulse for 2–3 seconds again to combine. Stir in the sesame seeds.

3. Season the salmon with a little kosher salt and freshly milled black pepper. Brush the Salmon fillets with the Dijon mustard and sprinkle to coat with the oat and nut mixture.

4. Place salmon on a baking tray and drizzle with a drizzle of good quality olive oil.

5. Bake until salmon is flakey and opaque in color, and this will take 12–15 minutes.

6. While the salmon is cooking, make the dressing by combining all the ingredients in a food blender and pulse until it is smooth. Prepare the garden salad greens in a bowl and combine with the dressing just before serving.

7. To serve, remove the skin from the salmon (that will easily pull away when cooked). Place the salmon in the center of each plate, with the dressed garden salad on the side.

Barmbrack Charm Bread

Serves 6–8

This name "brack" comes from the Irish word "breac" meaning speckled, the speckles are the fruits and candied peel. Traditionally, this sweet bread is eaten at Halloween with hidden charms baked in the bread including a ring (for love), money (for good fortune), a button (bachelor), a thimble (spinster), or a rag (poverty).

My mother used to wrap these charms in aluminum foil, and it was great family fun at Halloween, which might be one of the most famous Irish festivals celebrated across the world.

BREAD INGREDIENTS

4 cups of all-purpose flour (sifted)
1 teaspoon ginger
½ teaspoon cinnamon
¼ teaspoon nutmeg
¼ teaspoon of salt
½ cup soft brown sugar
4½ teaspoons of dry active yeast (2 packets)
4 ounces unsalted butter
1¼ cups of warm milk
1 egg (beaten)
1 cup of golden sultanas (golden raisins)
1 cup of dried currants
¼ cup of candied orange or lemon peel
   (finely chopped)

GLAZE INGREDIENTS

1 tablespoon sugar
1 tablespoon warm water

HOW TO MAKE

1. Butter a 9-inch round cake pans and set aside.

2. Measure and combine all the dry ingredients in a large bowl including the flour, spices, salt brown sugar, dry active yeast and the dried fruits and candied peel.

3. Combine all the wet ingredients in electric bread mixer including the warm milk, melted butter and egg. Slowly add the dry ingredients 1 cup at a time and mix to combine.

4. Transfer the sticky dough into the prepared pan and pat the dough in place. Cover with a clean dish towel and set aside in a warm place for about an hour for the dough to rise.

5. Preheat the oven to 375°F and then bake for about 30 minutes (to test the bread insert a skewer in the center and should come away clean).

6. Dissolve the sugar in boiling water to make the glaze and brush over the bread. Return the bread to the oven for a further few minutes until the loaf is glistening.

7. Transfer to a rack to cool and serve with Irish creamery butter.

Sweet & Spicy Hot Cross Buns

Makes 12 buns

This legendary recipe dates to the 12th century when it was eaten after Lent, the 40 days before Easter and often eaten on Good Friday. Over the centuries, the bun has also become symbolic of friendship and in the sharing of a hot cross bun, a famous rhyme says, "Half for you and half for me, between us two, good luck shall be." Another song we used to sing as children was "Hot Cross Buns Hot Cross Buns, One a Penny, Two a Penny, Hot Cross Buns."

Another firm favorite in Ireland in spring, baked as Easter approached, and I always loved the wonderful aroma of the sweet and spicy buns as they baked in the oven.

BUN INGREDIENTS

4 cups of all-purpose flour (sifted)
¼ cup of fine granulated sugar
2 teaspoons of mixed spice (cinnamon, nutmeg, cloves)
4½ teaspoons dry active yeast
2 large eggs (lightly beaten)
2 teaspoons vanilla extract
¾ teaspoon salt
1 cup seedless raisins
½ cup mixed peel
1¼ cup milk
4 tablespoons of butter

CROSS PASTE INGREDIENTS

½ cup all-purpose flour
5–6 tablespoons of water

SUGAR GLAZE INGREDIENTS

5 tablespoons of water
2 tablespoons of fine granulated sugar

HOW TO MAKE

1. Combine the flour, sugar, mixed spice, yeast, raisins, and mixed peel in a large bowl of mixer. Place the milk and 3 tablespoons of butter in a small saucepan and warm over low heat until the butter has melted. Combine the dry ingredients with the warm milk and butter and the beaten eggs to form slightly sticky dough. Knead the dough until it is smooth and elastic, about 5 minutes. Shape into a ball.

2. Brush the inside of a large bowl with the remaining 1 tablespoon butter. Put dough into bowl, turning to coat lightly with butter. Cover with plastic wrap. Let rise at room temperature until doubled in size, about 1 hour. The dough can be made the night before and allowed to rise in the refrigerator overnight.

3. To form the rolls, butter a 9 x 13-inch pan. Turn the dough out of the bowl and using a bench scrapper divide in to 12 equal portions, about 2 ounces each.

4. Tuck the edges of the dough under to make round rolls and place them seam-side down in the prepared pan, leaving a little space in between each roll. Set aside in a warm place until the rolls rise doubled in size, about 25–30 minutes.

5. Meanwhile, position the rack in the center of the oven and preheat to 375°F.

6. Mix the flour and water to make a paste and spoon into a small piping bag. Pipe a cross shape over each bun.

7. Bake rolls until golden brown and, about 20–25 minutes. Remove from oven and cool on a cooling rack.

8. To make the glaze, melt the sugar in water until it has dissolved and using a pastry brush paint each bun until glossy.

9. To serve, slice in half and spread with Irish creamery butter.

Wee Iced Fingers

A legendary northern Irish treat made famous by the Belfast song called "My Aunt Jane" who mentions childhood reflections on eating a bap with sugar on the top and drinking tea. The words are "she gave me tea out of her wee tin. Half a bap with sugar on top, three black lumps out of her wee shop."

If you cannot wait to sample these local delights, here is the 'wee' recipe!

DOUGH INGREDIENTS

4 fluid ounces (½ cup) warm water
⅔ cup warm milk
3 tablespoons unsalted butter, softened
2 eggs (beaten)
2 teaspoons salt
3⅔ cups all-purpose white flour
2 tablespoons yeast
¼ cup of fine granulated sugar

ICING INGREDIENTS

1½ cups powdered sugar
5 teaspoons cold water
1 drop of pink food coloring
⅓ cup pecans (chopped)
2 tablespoons dried coconut

FILLING INGREDIENTS

1½ cups heavy whipping cream
2 tablespoons fine granulates sugar
1 tablespoon vanilla
3 ounces strawberry jam

TOPPING INGREDIENTS

¼ cup unsweetened coconut and chopped
  toasted pecans

HOW TO MAKE

1. Combine the water, milk and butter in a small saucepan and heat until the butter has melted. Measure the flour, yeast, and sugar together. Using a flat bladed knife to mix add the wet ingredients including the beaten eggs, water, milk, and butter to the dry ingredients. If you have a bread hook attachment place on the lowest speed and allow ingredients to mix for amount 2–3 minutes.

2. Place the dough on to a lightly floured surface and knead for about 5 minutes or until smooth. Place the dough in a bowl and allow to rise for 45 minutes until it has almost doubled in size (or leave overnight in refrigerator to rise).

3. Preheat the oven to 425°F.

4. Divide the dough in to 24 pieces, and then roll into balls and shape in to fingers about 5-inches long. Then place the dough fingers on to a greased baking sheet, leaving them to double in size, set aside in a warm place for about 40 minutes.

5. Bake for 7–9 minutes or until lightly browned. Once baked remove from the oven and set on a baking rack to cool.

6. To ice the buns, sift the powdered sugar bowl and gradually stir in the cold water to form a thick paste and a small drop of pink food coloring.

7. Whip the cream until it forms stiff peaks and stir in the sugar and vanilla. Spoon into a piping bag.

8. To assemble the fingers slice them horizontally, leaving one long edge intact. Using a knife spread a little jam inside each sliced bun and then pipe whipped cream into each finger. Finally, using a knife or flat spreader, ice each bun. Sprinkle with unsweetened coconut and chopped pecans.

Grilled Oysters with an Irish Stout Herb Butter

Serves 4–6

Some say love is in the air, but in Ireland, love is in the oyster! Saint Brigid is said to have had a fondness for oysters, and the legend is told about a young girl who came to St. Brigid for help. A powerful druid was demanding the return of an exquisite missing pearl, and just as the young girl was pleading her case to Brigid, her maidservant came with a plate of oysters for dinner. When the Saint opened the first oyster shell, she found the missing oyster, to buy the girls freedom. The discovery of the pearl allowed the girl to marry the man she genuinely loved!

So, oysters are the thing, and this recipe is one of my favorites, good enough for St. Brigid herself, I think!

OYSTER INGREDIENTS

2 dozen large fresh oysters on the half shell
½ cup of Parmesan cheese (finely grated)

GUINNESS BUTTER INGREDIENTS

1 cup of butter
1 cup of Guinness stout (reduced to 4 tablespoon)
1 teaspoon sugar
1 tablespoon vegetable oil
2 tablespoons shallots (finely chopped)
2 garlic cloves (crushed)
1 teaspoon thyme (finely chopped)
2 tablespoons parsley (finely chopped)
1 teaspoon of kosher salt
½ teaspoon freshly ground black pepper

HOW TO MAKE

1. Prepare oysters using an oyster knife and shucking severing the muscle that is attaching the oyster to the shell. Leave the oyster in the shell that is more cupped shaped.
2. In a small saucepan simmer the Guinness, sugar, and thyme until it has reduced by 75 percent (leaving 4 tablespoons of liquid) and cool.
3. To make the Guinness butter, sauté the shallot in 1 tablespoon of vegetable oil for a few minutes to soften and then add the garlic at the end and cook for 1 minute.
4. Whip the room temperature butter by hand or with electric whisk and add the cooled reduced Guinness, parsley, shallots and garlic, salt, and pepper.
5. Preheat the fire or grill to 400–475°F.
6. Arrange the oysters in a single layer on a grill and spoon 2 teaspoons of the butter mixture into each oyster shell and then top with finely grated Dubliner Irish cheese. Grill uncovered for 6–7 minutes until the butter is sizzling and the oyster is puffed up.
7. Remove from the grill and serve immediately.

Colcannon Potatoes

The Gaelic term, *cal ceannann,* means "white headed cabbage" and it is a traditional Irish dish made by combining mashed potatoes with cabbage or kale. The different variety of cabbages available in Ireland, from the spring green to the autumnal variety, allows this dish to be made all year around.

Colcannon certainly is in the running for the national dish of Ireland, maybe pipped to the post by lamb stew, but just try both of these recipes and see what you think!

COLCANNON WITH SAVOY CABBAGE

2½ pounds potatoes (floury white skin variety)
1 pound of Savoy cabbage (cored and finely cut)
1 tablespoon vegetable oil
4 slices of thick cut bacon
4 fluid ounces (½ cup) whole milk
5 tablespoons salted butter (melted)
1 teaspoon of sea salt
½ teaspoons freshly ground black pepper

HOW TO MAKE

1. Peel and quarter potatoes. Place them in a large pan of salted water and cook in enough cold water to cover the potatoes for 30 minutes or until tender.

2. Drain the potatoes, cover the pan, and allow them to dry for a few minutes.

3. While the potatoes are still cooking, combine the melted butter and whole milk.

4. Finely slice the Savoy cabbage (chiffonade).

5. Slice the bacon into neat lardoons. In a large skillet heat a little canola oil and then sauté the bacon to crispy. Add the Savoy cabbage and cook for a few minutes.

6. Pass the potatoes through a moulin. Add the potatoes to the bacon and cabbage mixture. Stir in the cream mixture and taste to adjust seasonings.

COLCANNON WITH GREEN CABBAGE

2 pounds of red skinned potatoes
¾ cup of milk
6 tablespoons butter
1 cup of chopped onion
6 cups of shredded green cabbage
Sea salt and pepper

HOW TO MAKE

1. Cover and place the potatoes in a pan of cold salted water and boil until fork tender. Drain the potatoes and allow them to dry out a little. Mash the potatoes with the skins on.

2. In a clean skillet melt the butter and sauté the onion until soft and then stir in the cabbage and cook for just a few minutes until it is soft and fragrant.

3. Stir the cabbage and onion mixture in with the hot potatoes. Season with salt and pepper.

Saint Nicholas Sweet Mince Pies

These crumbly and decadent pies are Santa's favorite treats, and Irish children leave them out on Christmas Eve for him to enjoy by the chimney, just as American kids leave cookies. My children always loved these, and they are always a large part of our Irish Christmas.

Just as the name suggests, over the centuries the original recipe would have included meat as a filling, but today's mince pies fillings have been transformed to festive dried winter fruits, citrus, nuts, and spices, or sweet mince pies. You may want to double up the pastry recipe!

PASTRY INGREDIENTS

9 ounces all-purpose flour
1 ounce powdered sugar
¼ cup ground almonds
½ teaspoon salt
6 ounces unsalted butter (or 3 ounces of margarine and 3 ounces butter)
½ tablespoon of egg yolk (beaten)
1½ to 2 tablespoons ice water
½ tablespoon lemon juice
6 ounces mincemeat (recipe below)
Powdered sugar (to sprinkle)

SWEET MINCEMEAT INGREDIENTS

2 ounces currants
2 ounces raisins
2 ounces sultanas
2 ounces dried apricots (chopped)
2 ounces glazed cherries (chopped)
2 ounce fruit and peel mix
½ ounce chopped almonds
2 ounces soft brown sugar
2 tablespoons butter (melted)
½ teaspoon ground cloves
½–1 teaspoon cinnamon
½ teaspoon mixed spice
½ teaspoon ground ginger
3 tablespoons orange juice (plus the zest of one orange)
2 tablespoons of brandy
2 tablespoons of sherry

HOW TO MAKE

1. To make the mincemeat, stir all the ingredients together in a large bowl. If made in advance it can be stored in sterilized jars for up to 2 months.

2. To make the mince pies preheat the oven to 425°F.

3. Combine the flour, salt, and powdered sugar in a large bowl. Add in the ground almonds. Rub in the butter and margarine until it resembles breadcrumbs.

4. Blend the egg yolk, lemon juice and the water together and gradually add to the dry ingredients, until just enough to hold together.

5. Turn the pastry on to a lightly floured board and knead lightly. Cover the pastry and put aside in the fridge to relax for at least an hour or overnight.

6. Roll out the pastry very thin and using a pastry cutter cut in to 2-inch rounds. Spoon 1 teaspoon of mincemeat on to half the rounds. Brush edges all around with cold water. Place another on top and press edges together. Prick with a fork.

7. Bake for about 9 minutes until the pastry is golden brown. Allow to cool in the pan for a few minutes and then place mince pies on a cooling rack.

8. Sprinkle with powdered sugar.

Gran's Armagh Apple Creams

❧ *Makes 18 creams* ☙

St. Patrick is said to have planted several apple trees on his travels, including one at *Ceangoba* a settlement close to Armagh where I grew up. County Armagh in the springtime is filled with a sea of breathtaking pink blossoms which in time give way to those wonderful apples we enjoyed, including the Bramley, a variety of apple from Armagh, known for its tart flavor.

Today the Armagh Apple Blossom Festival in April is a firm favorite on the foodie calendar with tours of local orchards like Long Meadow a popular annual tradition—followed by a cider/juice tasting, of course!

My wee Gran perfected the recipe for these creams and the pastry here is rather like shortbread and ideal for fruit, custard, or chocolate fillings. These versatile little shells can be made in advance and stored in an airtight container for up to two weeks.

SEMOLINA PASTRY INGREDIENTS

1 cup plain flour
½ cup ground semolina flour
2 tablespoons fine granulated sugar
Pinch of salt
½ cup unsalted butter
2 tablespoons beaten egg (to bind dough)

APPLE FILLING INGREDIENTS

1½ cups chopped apples (peeled with cores removed)
3 tablespoons water
1 tablespoon lemon juice
2 tablespoons sugar

CREAM TOPPING INGREDIENTS

¼ cup heavy whipping cream (beaten)
1 teaspoon of cinnamon

HOW TO MAKE

1. To make the pastry, put the all-purpose and semolina flour, fine granulated sugar and salt in a food processor and pulse a few times to combine.

2. Cut the butter in to small pieces and pulse until the butter is incorporated to the consistency of breadcrumbs. Slowly add the beaten egg, a little at a time until the dough holds together.

3. Transfer the dough to the counter and work it together with hands and roll it into a ball. Cover and refrigerate for 15 minutes.

4. Preheat the oven to 300°F.

5. Roll out pastry on to a lightly floured surface. Using a round pastry cutter cut the shells and place into individual tart tins (2-inches top and ½-inch deep).

6. Bake for 20–25 minutes until the pastry is golden. Transfer the tart pan to a rack and leave them in the tin to cool for a few minutes before easing out on to a cooling rack.

7. To make the apple filling, combine the apples, water, sugar, and lemon juice in a medium saucepan. Cook the apples for 10–15 minutes until the apples are soft. Set aside to cool. To serve, place a teaspoon of apple sauce in each shell. Spoon whipped cream on top of the apple sauce and sprinkle with a little cinnamon.

Heaney's Hedgerow Pavlova

An Irish classic dessert with lime curd, crunchy meringue with a perfectly gooey inside, topped with blackberries from the Hedgerows.

In Ireland, the time to pick blackberries is September, when the hedges are filled with bursting berries begging to be picked. I recall the Ulster Poet Seamus Heaney when he writes in his poem "Blackberry picking," *"You at that first one and its flesh was sweet Like thickened wine: summer's blood was in it."*

MERINGUE INGREDIENTS

4 egg whites (at room temperature)
1⅓ cups extra-fine sugar
1½ teaspoons cornstarch
1½ teaspoons distilled white vinegar
1 vanilla bean (split lengthwise) or 2 teaspoons
  of vanilla extract
Pinch of salt

TOPPING INGREDIENTS

½ cup heavy whipping cream (1 cup whipped)
2 teaspoons extra fine sugar
1½ cups blackberries (washed)
¼ cup of balsamic vinegar (reduced to 1 tablespoon)

LIME CURD INGREDIENTS

¾ cup granulated sugar
3 large eggs (beaten)
½ cup of lime juice
4 tablespoons unsalted butter (room temperature)
Zest of 3 small limes
Pinch of salt

HOW TO MAKE

1. To make the lime curd, place all the beaten eggs, sugar, lime juice and zest together over a double boiler and stir together on low heat to cook for 5 minutes, or until the curd is thick enough to coat the back of a spoon. Whisk in the butter a little bit at a time and add a pinch of salt. Strain the curd into a clean bowl. Set aside in the refrigerator to cool.

2. Preheat the oven to 300°F.

3. Line and grease a baking sheet with parchment wax paper.

4. In an electric mixer beat the egg whites at room temperature. Slowly incorporate sugar one teaspoons at a time. Blend in the cornstarch, vinegar, and vanilla.

5. Spread the meringue in a circular fashion on a lined baking sheet, building up the edges a little higher than the middle.

6. Place the pavlova in the oven and then reduce it down to 250°F. to bake low and slow. Bake the pavlova for 1¼ hours and then switch off the oven allowing the pavlova to dry out for another hour so that it becomes crunchier on the outside but still maintains a lovely soft center.

7. Whip the fresh cream, sugar and vanilla until thick peaks appear.

8. To assemble the pavlova, spoon the top with lime curd, then add the whipped fresh cream, and finally decorate with the blackberries on top.

Celtic Chocolate Yule Log

The Ancient Celts would gather as part of the Winter Solstice festivities, signaling winter's end and the days finally becoming longer, cleansing the air of the previous year's events. To usher in the Spring, families would burn logs decorated with holly, pinecones, or ivy. Wine and salt were also often used to anoint the logs. Once burned, the logs ashes were valuable treasures and said to have medicinal benefits to guard against evil.

With the event of Christianity, the Yule log tradition continued, albeit on a smaller scale. Families may have burned a log on Christmas Eve, but with smaller hearths. We do not know who exactly made the first Yule log cake, but we know it was inspired by the Celts!

SPONGE INGREDIENTS

6 large eggs (room temperature)
1 cup fine granulated sugar
1 cup cake flour or all-purpose flour (sifted)
½ cup cocoa powder (sifted)
2 tablespoons hot water

CHOCOLATE FUDGE ICING

11.5 ounces of semi-sweet chocolate
1 cup heavy whipping cream
1 teaspoon unsalted butter
1¾ cups powdered sugar

VANILLA CREAM FILLING

1 cup heavy whipping cream
½ teaspoon vanilla
2 tablespoons granulated white sugar

HOW TO MAKE

1. Preheat the oven to 400°F.

2. Prepare a 10 x 15-inch jelly roll pan by lining with parchment paper and lightly greasing to prevent the cake from sticking.

3. Using electric mixer beat the eggs and sugar together until it is frothy, pale yellow in color and the consistency is thick enough to leave a trail.

4. Gently fold in the flour and cocoa powder and finally the warm water.

5. Spread resulting mixture in to prepared baking sheet and bake for about 8–10 minutes.

6. While cake is baking, prepare a thin, clean kitchen towel and sprinkle it with powdered sugar.

7. Place the baked sponge upside down on to the prepared kitchen towel and gently peel off the wax paper and discard it. Then, slowly roll up the cake and the towel together. Set aside on a wire rack to cool.

8. To prepare the chocolate icing, heat heavy whipping cream, chocolate, and butter over a double boiler. Transfer chocolate ganache to an electric mixer and add the powdered sugar to make the chocolate fudge icing mixing until smooth.

9. To prepare cream filling, beat heavy whipping cream, vanilla, and sugar until stiff.

10. To assemble chocolate log cake, unroll the sponge and remove the paper. Using a spatula fill with the fresh cream.

11. Roll up the log and trim the edges with a knife. Cut a short diagonal wedge of one end to resemble a branch and sandwich them together with the reserved cream and peaches mixture.

12. Using a knife dipped in warm water cover the log with chocolate icing. Swirl icing with a fork to resemble a bark of a tree.

13. Dust with icing sugar to resemble snow and add a Christmas red ornamental bird for festive fun.

A Toast to Ireland, Slainte!

Irish foods and drinks made with whiskey, beer and more

The City of Dublin has over a thousand years of history, matched only by her thousand pubs all offering a welcome toast of our Irish whiskies, beers and spirits. Pubs form the social fabric of many Irish communities, and all over the world there are Irish pubs which are creating the same needed social framework. It never ceases to amaze us that no matter where we travel in the world there will be an Irish pub of some sort literally everywhere, from South America to Asia. Almost every town we have visited in America had an Irish watering hole and it is clear that the Irish diaspora needed that critical social network provided by the pub.

Things have moved on from the Boston lonely boarding houses where Irish emigrants faced evenings of solitude after a long day's work far from home, but still, the Irish pub is a home away from home for many a lonely heart.

Irish settlers in America, as I am sure Etta and John did, found great comfort in the safety of the familiar pub in an unfamiliar land. We certainly did, and still do. We love our local Irish pubs here in America. We love the network of Irish American life that stems from them, from rugby games to the annual Saint Patrick's Day celebration, which can get quite elaborate! My heart swells with emotion each year to see the wearing of the green, and millions of Americans of Irish ancestry celebrating their cultural identity. How incredible it is to see the Chicago River being dyed green to commemorate the saint that introduced Christianity to Ireland, whilst in Savannah, their 200-year-old celebration includes dying the fountain In Forsyth Square green as almost a half a million people from across the country flood the streets clad in Irish regalia, each one with an Irish inspired beverage in hand whether that be a green beer or an Irish whiskey.

The very first St. Patrick's Day parade was held on March 17, 1601, in St. Augustine, Florida in a Spanish colony, organized by the local Irish vicar and America has been raising a glass to the saint himself and to all things Irish ever since!

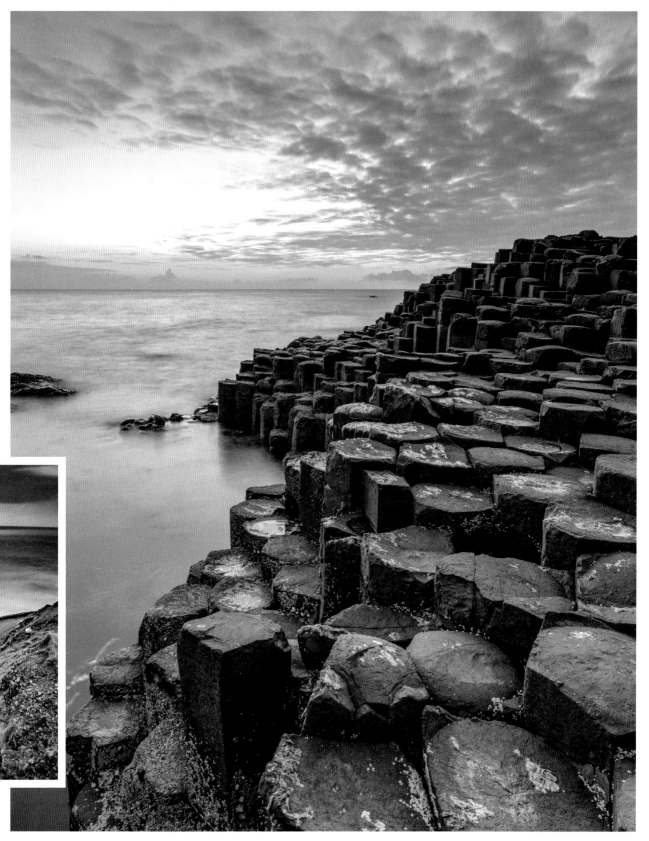

The Water of Life

Irish whiskey is one of the world's fastest growing spirits and to meet the ever-growing demand worldwide, new distilleries are emerging throughout the island of Ireland, from the Northern Coast to the Dingle Peninsula. The earliest record of whiskey, also known as 'Uisce Beatha', or 'the water of life', is recorded in 1405 in the *Annals of Clonmacnoise*. Despite this though, we do know that whiskey has an older tradition with monks, who have been distilling whiskey in the small monastic settlements from centuries earlier.

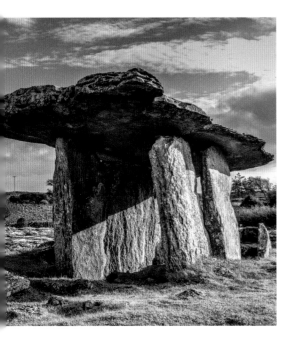

Ireland, as I have mentioned, is chock full of whiskey distilleries, such as the Old Bushmills Distillery in County Antrim which claims to be the oldest licensed Distillery in the world, with its registration being signed by King James I in 1603. Then, there is maybe the most famous distillery tour experience in Ireland: Jameson's in Middleton, County Cork, which is an absolute gem with its multiple brands and stories! There is just something about walking around those old original buildings, when you can feel the history dancing on the walls, or maybe that is just the effects coming from the tasting rooms! Newer distilleries such as Echlinville in County Down are resurrecting traditional brands such as Dunville's while the poitin makers at Micil have laid down the first whiskey in Galway for more than 100 years.

Glendalough Distillery was founded by five friends in the Wicklow Mountains, born from a passion for bringing Irish whiskey distilling back to its traditional roots. In recent years, the distilling of gin has become extremely popular. Glendalough distilleries just south of Dublin source botanicals hand-foraged from the Wicklow Mountains, themselves known as the 'Garden of Ireland'. Their award-winning Wild Botanical Gin reflects a mix of plants that are gathered during each of the four seasons.

The brewing of beer has a long history in Ireland, although it was originally brewed without hops, as the hop plant so popular in craft beers today is not native to Ireland. The bestselling Irish beer today is of course Guinness, founded by Arthur Guinness in 1759. Visitors can visit the brewery at St. James Gate and learn how to pour the perfect pint, which can be quite a feat! In addition to the more established brands of beer, smaller microbreweries are springing up offering malty chocolate stouts and interesting flavors. Whitewater Brewery in Castlewellan in County Down won a Golden Fork for its Krema de la Kremlin Russian stout aged in a whiskey cask while Nigel Logan at Hillstown Brewery economusee in County Antrim feeds the leftovers from the brewing to his herd of cows. Chefs across the island use these brews in their dishes and beer pairings are almost as popular as wine pairings. Caroline Hennessy from Eight Degrees Brewing in Cork recommends simple grilled fish or barbecued chicken kebabs to go with their malt stout and Cooleeney cheese to accompany the Sunburnt Red Ale.

We have included a selection of both desserts infused with our favorite drinks, and a few of our favorite cocktails. So, I raise a glass to my Irish ancestors who paved the way by setting both old and new traditions in a New World, and I am refreshed by the sacrifices, and drink deeply from that well. I raise a glass to the future generations, that I may leave a legacy worthy of following.

Slainte!

CHAPTER EIGHT
Whiskeys and More

*Irish Cream Cheesecake
with a Salted Caramel Sauce*
(page 212)

Irish Stout Chocolate Cake with a Cream Cheese Icing

Serves 8

When we go home to Ireland, it is always a celebration. We may be careful about desserts throughout the year, but when we are back in Ireland, we make sure to enjoy our food to the fullest and not skip the sweet stuff!

Many of our favorite pubs and coffee shops back home feature this delicious stout cake, and after trying it on tour, I could not wait to replicate it at home. As a result, it is now one of my family's favorite cakes. The cake has an intense chocolate flavor, though not overly sweet. It is a flavor that lingers with the taste of Irish stout, always a delight to end a celebratory meal.

The natural chocolate flavor in the stout is perfect in this recipe, and the fluffy Irish cream icing adds to the decadence. It is also one of those easy, never fail recipes worthy of any celebration or family gathering.

CAKE INGREDIENTS

1 cup Irish stout
5 ounces (10 tablespoons) unsalted butter (room temperature)
2 cups light brown sugar
⅔ cup unsweetened cocoa
2 large eggs (beaten)
¾ cup of sour cream
2 cups of all-purpose flour
2½ teaspoons baking soda (sifted)
½ teaspoon of salt

ICING INGREDIENTS

4 ounces cream cheese (room temperature)
2 ounces (4 tablespoons) unsalted butter
2½ cups of powdered sugar
3 tablespoons Irish cream liquor

GARNISH

1 ounce chocolate (shaved)

HOW TO MAKE

1. Preheat the oven to 350°F. Grease and line a 9-inch springform style pan with parchment paper and set aside.

2. Combine the stout and butter in a small saucepan and heat until the butter has melted, whisking to combine. Remove from the heat and stir in the sugar and cocoa powder whisking to combine and no lumps remain. Set aside to cool.

3. Measure the flour, baking soda and salt together.

4. Beat the eggs and sour cream together by hand or with an electric mixer. Add the cooled chocolate Irish stout mixture and beat on low speed to combine. Finally, add the dry ingredients one tablespoon at a time until fully incorporated. Pour the batter in to the lined springform pan.

5. Bake the cake for 45–50 minutes until it has risen. To test if the cake is done, place a skewer in the center of the cake and it should come out clean. Cool the cake on a wire rack.

6. To make the icing, whip the cream cheese and butter together until they are light and fluffy. Add the powdered sugar and the Irish cream whipping together until it is smooth.

7. Remove the cake from the springform pan and place on a serving plate. Using a spatula, smooth the icing over the cake.

8. Decorate with chocolate shavings.

Irish Cream Cheesecake with a Salted Caramel Sauce

The Irish are a people that most definitely have a sweet tooth, and in our family, we love to end a good meal with a mouthwatering dessert. My grandmother always had a sweet trolley brimming with cakes and sweet things at her guest house when she entertained, which means dessert baking is very much in my veins.

Cheesecake is a rich, creamy comfort food, and this boozy Irish version is silky smooth and dense, with a touch of Irish cream. After all, we would not be Irish if we did not find a way to add whiskey into the mix somewhere!

Baking these special Irish cheesecakes in individual jars makes for a fun presentation and allows guests not only to pour their own measure of dreamy burnt caramel sauce, but also to be transported straight back to the Emerald Isle.

CRUST INGREDIENTS

½ cup graham cracker crumbs or British digestive biscuits
2 tablespoons granulated sugar
1½ ounces (3 tablespoons) butter (melted)

CHEESECAKE LAYER INGREDIENTS

6 ounces cream cheese (room temperature)
1 tablespoon granulated sugar
5½ fluid ounces (½ cup) sweetened condensed milk
1 large egg (beaten)
1 teaspoon cornstarch
1½ tablespoons Irish cream
1 teaspoon vanilla extract
2 tablespoons sour cream

TOFFEE SAUCE INGREDIENTS

3 tablespoons granulated sugar
2 tablespoons unsalted butter (cut in cubes)
½ cup heavy whipping cream
Pinch of sea salt

HOW TO MAKE

1. For the graham cracker crust layer combine the crushed graham crackers, sugar and butter and mix well. Press 2½ tablespoon into the bottom of 4 (8-ounce) mason jars.

2. Preheat the oven to 350°F. Place the jars in a 9 x 13-inch pan and bake for 10 minutes. Remove from the oven and cool slightly while preparing the batter.

3. For the cheesecake layer, beat the cream cheese and sugar with an electric mixer until very fluffy. Add the condensed milk, sour cream, cornstarch, Irish cream and vanilla. Add the eggs one at a time, beating well and scraping the bowl after each addition. Beat on high for two more minutes.

4. Divide the batter among prepared jars, about ½ cup in each jar and return jars in to the 9 x 13-inch pan. Add enough water to pan to fill the pan ½ full. Bake at 350°F for 30 minutes. Remove from the oven and allow jars to cool to room temperature.

5. To make the burnt caramel, heat the sugar on a wide based skillet on medium high heat, allowing it to melt. Do not stir to prevent the sugar crystallizing and allow it to burn slightly for 1 minute. Stir in the cubed butter a little at a time. Finally whisk in the cream.

6. To serve the cheesecakes, serve the burnt toffee sauce on the side.

Owen Brennan's Bananas Foster

Serves 4

New Orleans is famous for its Creole and French cuisine, but many may not know about one of its most famous recipes being accredited to the Brennan family, of Irish decent. Bananas Foster was invented in 1951 when the New Orleans Irish American Restaurateur, Owen Brennan asked his chef to invent a recipe to give to a magazine. The results became an international sensation!

BANANA FOSTER INGREDIENTS

2 ounces (¼ cup) unsalted Irish butter
1 cup of dark brown sugar
¼ teaspoon cinnamon
⅛ teaspoon nutmeg
¼ cup dark rum
¼ cup banana liqueur
Pinch of Fleur de Sel (or other fine sea salt)
4 medium size bananas (sliced)

SERVING INGREDIENTS

4 generous scoops of vanilla ice cream

HOW TO MAKE

1. In a large skillet combine the butter, sugar, cinnamon, and Fleur de Sel, cinnamon and gently heat on a low temperature until the sugar dissolves.

2. Whisk in the banana liqueur and then add bananas to pan and cook for 2 minutes or until they begin to caramelize.

3. Stir in the rum and cook for 1 minute. Stand back and then tilt the pan to ignite the alcohol.

4. To serve, place a generous scoop of vanilla ice cream inside a serving dish and then top with the caramelized banana mixture and resulting sauce. Serve right away!

Marmalade Bread Pudding
with Whiskey Orange Sauce

Bread pudding was a staple in our home through-out my childhood, and my mother, who was always inventive, used to make a lighter version for our family, substituting milk for heavy cream.

Each year at Halloween, we made *Barmbrack*, which is a type of traditional Irish bread, and the following day we made bread pudding with the leftovers. In this chapter, we are celebrating the best of Irish food, and with this more decadent version of the classic bread pudding, we have a dish worthy of a special occasion.

Orange marmalade always pairs well with whiskey, and it adds a citrus tang to an old Irish favorite dessert. You will find the Barmbrack bread recipe in the Legendary Ireland chapter of this book.

BREAD INGREDIENTS

12 ounces (340 g) loaf of Barmbrack bread, sliced 1½-inches thick) or substitute with Brioche bread
1 tablespoon of unsalted butter

CUSTARD INGREDIENTS

5 large eggs (beaten)
2 cups heavy whipping cream
½ cup sugar
1 tablespoon Irish whiskey
1 teaspoon vanilla
¼ teaspoon kosher salt
½ cup of orange marmalade (to glaze)

ORANGE WHISKEY SAUCE

2 eggs (lightly beaten)
½ cup orange juice (juice of 2 oranges with 1 teaspoon zest)
¾ cup of sugar
¼ cup of water
1 tablespoon unsalted butter
3–4 tablespoons Irish whiskey

HOW TO MAKE

1. Grease an 8 x 8-inch pan with 1 tablespoon of the room temperature butter. Cut the sliced loafs in triangles and arrange in a single layer in pan.

2. Whisk together the eggs, sugar and cream, whiskey, vanilla, and kosher salt and pour half the custard over the bread. Repeat with one layer of sliced bread triangles and pour over the remaining custard mixture pressing down with your hands to absorb the liquid. Cover and set aside to soak for at 1½–2 hours before baking (or leave overnight in the fridge).

3. Preheat oven to 350°F.

4. Bake the pudding for 45–50 minutes, covering it with foil for the first 40 minutes and then baked uncovered for the last 10 minutes until the custard is set and it is lightly brown. Heat the orange marmalade and brush over the top of the pudding using a pastry brush.

5. For a caramelized top switch, turn the broiler to high and allow the pudding to brown a little on the top for 2 minutes.

6. To make the orange whiskey sauce, combine the lightly beaten eggs, orange juice with zest, sugar, and water in a small saucepan. Gently cook on low and stir for 5 minutes until the sauce begins to thicken. Finally, whisk in the butter a little at a time and the Irish whiskey at the very end. Strain and pour into a jug and refrigerate the sauce until ready to serve.

7. To serve the pudding, cut and slice while still warm and pour the orange sauce.

Chocolate Brownie Soufflé with Irish Cream Sauce

Serves 6

This heavenly chocolate pudding will melt in your mouth, and it is surprisingly light. This recipe is my secret weapon for entertaining because you can make them ahead of time, freeze and bake straight from the freezer. Just remember to serve them straight away from the oven, so they do not deflate when pouring over the boozy ice cream sauce.

SOUFFLE INGREDIENTS

3 tablespoons granulated sugar (plus 2 tablespoons more for ramekins)
2 teaspoons cocoa
2 tablespoons unsalted butter (plus 2 tablespoons more for ramekins)
4 ounces bittersweet dark chocolate or semi-sweet chocolate chips
3 large egg yolks
4 large egg whites
3 tablespoons granulated sugar
2 tablespoons boiling water
⅛ teaspoon cream of tartar
Pinch of fine salt

VANILLA BEAN ICE CREAM SAUCE

½ cup of vanilla ice cream
4 tablespoons of heavy whipping cream (whipped)
4 tablespoons Irish cream (optional)

HOW TO MAKE

1. Brush six ramekins with softened unsalted Irish butter. Combine 2 tablespoons of sugar and cocoa and then coat evenly.

2. Melt the butter and chocolate together in a bowl set over a pan of simmering water.

3. Beat the egg yolks at medium speed in an electric mixer and gradually add the 3 tablespoons of sugar (that has been dissolved in 2 tablespoons of boiling water) for about 3 minutes or until thickened. Fold into the chocolate mixture with a pinch of sea salt.

4. Using clean whisks beat the egg whites and cream of tartar until foamy white peaks form (being careful not to over beat). Take in a few tablespoons of the egg white mixture and mix by hand to loosen the chocolate mixture. Gently fold in the remaining egg whites.

5. Spoon the mixture in to prepared ramekins. If freezing the soufflés, cover each ramekin with plastic wrap and place in the freezer.

6. When ready to serve, remove soufflés from the freezer 30 minutes before baking.

7. Preheat the oven to 400°F and bake until they are fully risen; 20–25 minutes if baking from frozen or 15 minutes when made to order and then baked. (Please note the soufflés will fall so they need to be eaten right away).

8. To make the sauce allow the ice cream to come to room temperature. Whip the cream and combine. Stir in the optional Irish cream.

9. To serve, pierce a little hole with the back of a dessert spoon and pour over the sauce.

Silky Irish Cream Brûlée

This luxurious and silky-smooth baked cream custard is the perfect ending to any meal. The toasted and slightly burnt crispy caramelized sugar on top cracks when open when tapped with a spoon, to unveil the glorious custard. Why not pair this with a wee dram on the side with its caramel notes that complement this brûlée.

BRÛLÉE INGREDIENTS

2 cups heavy cream
6 egg yolks (slightly beaten/room temperature)
⅓ cup sugar
3 tablespoons Irish cream liquor
1 teaspoon vanilla
Small pinch sea salt

BRÛLÉE TOPPING

6 tablespoons of extra fine sugar (and more if needed)

GARNISH

¼ cup fresh berries (to garnish)

HOW TO MAKE

1. Preheat oven to 325°F.

2. In a small heavy based saucepan, stir together the cream and sugar over medium-low heat to simmering or until the sugar has dissolved. Remove from the heat and add the Irish cream, vanilla and salt.

3. In a small bowl, whisk the egg yolks together.

4. Slowly whisk the warm cream mixture into the egg mixture being careful not to curdle by incorporating a few tablespoons at a time.

5. Place 6 ramekin dishes in a large deep dish baking pan. Pour custard mixture evenly into each dish. Fill the pan with enough boiling water to surround the ramekin dishes to halfway.

6. Bake the custards for 40–45 minutes or until the custard has set (as a test place a knife inside the center of the custard and it should come out clean when they are ready).

7. Remove custards from the oven and oven bath and allow cooling on a wire rack for at least an hour before refrigerating.

8. Before serving remove the custards from refrigerator.

9. Sprinkle 1 tablespoons of sugar evenly over each crème brûlée. Using a small handheld blow torch, begin to melt the sugar until it begins to caramelize and turn a deep brown color. (If you do not own a handheld blowtorch, the brûlée can caramelize underneath a broiler).

10. Serve immediately garnished with fresh berries.

Shamrock & Peach Signature Macaron

Makes 2 dozen cookies

This unique recipe was created for a Shamrock and Peach event by my friend Chef Chloe. The crunch of the delicate almond meringue shells and the fruit peach filling is an incredible combination.

In Ireland, these feature widely in post dinner petit four selection after dinner or part of an elegant afternoon tea. The ingredients should be measured using a digital measuring scale for these dainty cookies!

COOKIE INGREDIENTS

4 ounces (½ cup) almond flour
7 ounces confectioners' sugar
3 large egg whites (room temperature)
¼ teaspoon cream of tartar
2 ounces (¼ cup) granulated sugar
1 teaspoon Irish cream
Pinch of salt
Green food coloring

BUTTERCREAM FILLING INGREDIENTS

¼ cup butter, softened
2 ounces (¼ cup) cream cheese
3 tablespoons peach preserves
1 tablespoon Irish cream
2½ cups confectioner's sugar

HOW TO MAKE

1. Line two baking sheets with parchment paper. Prepare a pastry bag with a large round tip.
2. Using a food processor, pulse the powdered sugar and almond flour into a powder. Sift several times until there are little to no almond bits left.
3. In electric mixer, whisk egg whites, salt, and cream of tartar. Beat until egg white's foam. With mixer on medium high, add sugar 1–2 tablespoons at a time and continue until stiff peaks form.
4. Add in Irish cream and 1–2 drops of food coloring and beat for an additional minute to incorporate. Sift the almond flour and confectioner's sugar and gently fold into egg whites gradually.
5. Transfer batter into pastry bag and pipe onto baking sheet, making evenly sized circles.
6. Let shells sit for 20–30 minutes to dry. Check for a skin to form on the top of the cookie (should not stick to finger when touched)
7. Preheat oven to 300°F. Bake for 12–13 minutes or until shell has hardened. Be sure to rotate cookies halfway through baking.
8. Cool completely on cookie sheets before peeling from the parchment.
9. To make the buttercream icing, prepare the piping bag with a large round tip.
10. Beat together the butter and cream cheese until fluffy. Beat in the cooled peach purée and vanilla!
11. Add enough confectioner's sugar until desired piping has been reached. Transfer filling into the piping bag and pipe a small amount onto one cookie.
12. Top with another cookie to make the macaron sandwich.

Dark Chocolate Sea Salt Whiskey Truffle

For chocolate lovers like me, Ireland's gourmet handmade chocolatier cafés are a taste of heaven. Our exceptionally rich dairy, and the legendary pride we take in chocolate making, has put Ireland on the worldwide confectionary stage, with chocolate specialty shops throughout Dublin and the entire island.

Irish immigrants like myself typically have two requests from family when they visit us here in America: bring some Irish tea and bring some Irish chocolate. We can never seem to get enough of it.

Chocolate pairs well with Irish whiskey and scotch. Like food and wine, though, matching the two takes careful thought and depends on personal tastes. Whiskeys that have been matured in sherry and bourbon casks have a sweet aroma, with flavors such as vanilla, caramel and honey. More mature whiskeys have notes of fruitcake, candied fruits, and spices—flavors that really sing when paired with creamier chocolate.

Enjoy these truffles by themselves, with an Irish coffee, or paired with a glass of unpeated, aged whiskey.

TRUFFLE INGREDIENTS

1 cup heavy cream
3 tablespoons of Irish whiskey
12 ounces quality dark chocolate
4 ounces (½ cup) unsalted Irish butter (room temperature)
Pinch of Fleur de Sel (or other fine sea salt)
Cocoa powder (to roll truffles)

HOW TO MAKE

1. Preheat oven to 350°F.

2. Place the cream in a saucepan and bring to a low boil, reducing to 50 percent.

3. Stir in the chocolate until it has melted. Whisk in the Irish cream and then the softened butter until smooth and glossy.

4. Transfer chocolate mixture to a shallow pan and refrigerate until firm.

5. Using a melon ball scoop form balls and roll with hands and then toss in cocoa powder.

6. Best stored and served from the refrigerator.

Shamrock & Peach Summer Cocktail

 Makes 1 cocktail

This Shamrock and Peach signature cocktail is best enjoyed in summer when the homegrown peaches are in season. It has a delightful peach color and taste, and the basil garnish brings a lovely green herbal infusion. The final splash of the prosecco brings sparkle to this cocktail worthy of any celebratory occasion!

COCKTAIL BASE INGREDIENTS

1.5 ounces gin
1½ tablespoons peach preserves
1 ounce ginger simple syrup
1 ounce freshly squeezed lime juice
Prosecco (to top off the glass)
Sprig of basil (to garnish)

GINGER SIMPLE SYRUP INGREDIENTS

4 ounces fresh ginger root
1 cup sugar
1 cup water

HOW TO MAKE

1. To make the ginger syrup, remove the rough outer skin from the ginger root with a sharp knife and then slice thinly. The ginger syrup base makes up to eight drinks.

2. In a small saucepan, bring the sugar and water to a boil over medium high heat. Add the ginger and simmer for a few minutes to infuse. Remove from the heat and allow the ginger to continue to infuse for at least 45 minutes. Strain the syrup and refrigerate.

3. To make the cocktail, mix 1 ounce of the prepared ginger syrup with the gin, peach preserves, ginger and lime juice together using a shaker.

4. Strain into a glass with crushed ice and top with a little prosecco.

5. Garnish with a basil leaf.

Pot O' Gold with Apple & Gin

Makes 1 cocktail

Halloween was invented in Ireland, so fall celebrations are an important way to toast summer's end and usher in the golden hues of autumn and the upcoming winter holiday season. The Irish Gin industry is booming, and for good cause too! With a bouquet of botanicals, and citrus tasting notes, Irish gin is flavorful enough to still stand out, while remaining light enough to blend in cocktails.

COCKTAIL BASE INGREDIENTS

2 ounces gin
2 ounces freshly pressed apple cider
1 ounce apple pie honey syrup

APPLE PIE HONEY SYRUP

1 cup water (filtered)
2 Granny Smith green apples (cut with skin and seeds)
2 whole cloves
1 vanilla pod (split with seeds scraped)
2 sticks of cinnamon
½ cup honey

HOW TO MAKE

1. To make the apple pie honey syrup, place all the ingredients in a small saucepan and bring to a boil. Simmer for 5 minutes. Remove from the heat and allow to sit for at least 30 minutes (or overnight). Cool in the refrigerator, and strain into a clean jug. Syrup base makes up to eight drinks.

2. To make the cocktail, fill a shaker three quarters full of crushed ice.

3. Add 1 ounce of the prepared apple pie honey syrup as well as the gin and freshly pressed apple cider.

4. Cover and shake vigorously for 10–15 seconds.

5. To serve, fill a chilled glass with ice and the matchstick apples. Strain over the cocktail and then garnish with a spring of thyme.

Winter Solstice Fizz: Spiced Cranberry with Irish Whiskey & Rosemary

Makes 1 cocktail

The holiday season is one of merriment and what better way of toasting the season than enjoying this refreshing cocktail, featuring both cranberries and Irish whiskey? The winter solstice is about celebrating the festive colors of green and red, and the rich flavors of spices and rosemary.

COCKTAIL BASE INGREDIENTS

1.5 ounces Irish whiskey
1 tablespoon lime juice
2 tablespoons spiced cranberry syrup (see below)
Fever-Tree Indian Tonic Water or Club Soda water
    (enough to fill up the glass)

SPICED CRANBERRY SYRUP

1 cup of cranberries
1 cup of water
1 cup of sugar
1 cinnamon stick
1 rosemary stem
½-inch of sliced ginger root

GARNISH INGREDIENTS

Rosemary, cranberries, lime curl

HOW TO MAKE

1. To make the spiced cranberry syrup, place the sugar, water, cranberries, ginger root, rosemary and cinnamon stick in a saucepan and simmer together for 7–8 minutes. Cover and allow to sit for at least 2 hours, or even better overnight.

2. Strain the syrup into a clean jar after the flavors have had time to infuse. The syrup base makes up to eight drinks.

3. To serve, fill a glass with ice and add the whiskey, lime juice, cranberry syrup. Stir the glass to incorporate all the ingredients. Top off the glass with a little club soda.

4. Stir one more time and then garnish the cocktail. Suggested garnishes include a sprig of fresh rosemary, a few cranberries or lime curl, or a combination of all three.

  A RETURN TO IRELAND

Hot Toddy

The Irish cure for the cold symptoms never fails! When you are not feeling well, this old-fashioned recipe warms the heart and soul and just like a bowl of chicken soup is the soul, it is sure to bring comfort and relief and a real pick me up! Go ahead give it a go!

TODDY INGREDIENTS

1 tablespoon raw honey
1 tablespoon fresh lemon juice
1 lemon peel twist
4 cloves
Boiling water
2 ounces Irish whiskey

HOW TO MAKE

1. Prepare the lemon twist by studding with cloves and set aside.

2. Warm up a glass by filling it with boiling water and then discarding. Add the honey and lemon juice to the glass and then pour boiling water filling the glass half full. Stir to dissolve the honey and the add the lemon and clove twist.

3. Finally, top with the Irish whiskey and gently stir. Enjoy!

Irish Eggnog

When the holiday's roll around there is nothing like a toast of eggnog shared with close family and friends! Hope you enjoy our Irish-style toast!

EGGNOG INGREDIENTS

8 eggs (beaten)
1 cup sugar
3 cups milk
3 cups heavy whipping cream
1 teaspoon ground nutmeg
½ cup Irish whiskey

HOW TO MAKE

1. In a large saucepan, combine the eggs, sugar, 1 cup of milk and 1 cup of cream. Cook and stir over medium heat for about 10 minutes or until the thermometer reads 140°F or is thick enough to coat the back of a metal spoon.

2. Remove from the heat and pour into a large bowl. Stir in nutmeg and the remaining milk and cream. Place bowl in an ice water bath, stir frequently until mixture is cool. Cover and refrigerate for at least 3 hours before serving.

3. Stir in the whiskey to the egg mixture using a metal whisk. Enjoy!

Boozy Cookie Butter Chocolate Milkshake

For a grown-up party, there is nothing as fun and delicious as a boozy milkshake. We have added cookie butter to the chocolate ice cream and Guinness for extra decadence! If you have never tried cookie butter before, it is basically ground up cookies in a jar, with the consistency of nut butter. Very naughty, but nice!

MILKSHAKE INGREDIENTS

1 pint (4 cups) chocolate ice cream
1 cup Guinness Irish stout
½ cup cookie butter

CREAM TOPPING INGREDIENTS

½ cup heavy cream (makes 1 cup whipped)
1 tablespoon pure cane sugar

GARNISH

1 tablespoon chocolate curls

HOW TO MAKE

1. In a blender, combine the Guinness, ice cream and cookie butter, and blend on low until smooth (you can add a little Guinness depending on your preferred consistency).

2. Divide the mixture between 4 small or two large glasses.

3. Whip the cream and sugar and spoon it on top of the milkshake. The cream topping will serve up to 4–6 drinks.

4. Garnish with chocolate shavings and enjoy!

Red Branch Knights

This deep ruby red Irish whiskey cocktail deserves a fit for royal name! The flavors are fruity and bold and can be served as an after-dinner cocktail.

The Red Branch Knights of the Fianna were a group of elite warriors who were in the service of Concobar MacNessa, who was the King of Ulster. The King ruled from Emain Macha (Armagh) that was a seat of royalty and a place of legends. Slainte!

COCKTAIL BASE INGREDIENTS

1½ ounces Irish whiskey
¾ ounce cabernet syrup
¾ ounce lemon juice
1 egg white

CABERNET SYRUP INGREDIENTS

1 cup cabernet red wine
1 cup granulated sugar

GARNISH

Lemon peel

HOW TO MAKE

1. To make the cabernet simple syrup, combine equal parts wine to sugar in a saucepan and simmer for 7–8 minutes, or until the sugar has dissolved. Remove from the heat and store in the refrigerator until you are ready to make the cocktail. This base makes up to eight drinks.

2. To assemble the cocktail, place ice in a shaker and then add the whiskey, lemon juice, the egg white, and 1 ounce of cabernet syrup. Shake vigorously.

3. Pour into a martini style glass (the egg white separate to form a foamy head).

4. Garnish the side of the glass with the lemon curl. To make the lemon curl, use a knife to trim the ends of a lemon. Cut a slice of lemon horizontally to make a ring from it. Use a knife to cut around the inside flesh and white pith to leave the yellow peel (you may need to go over the peel with a paring knife a second time to remove any remaining pith). Use the edge of a straw or just twist the peel to a curly q shape, and it should hold its shape.

Black Velvet Cocktail

Why not add a little sparkle in to your Guinness, by adding champagne? The Black velvet is a special cocktail made with equal parts champagne, Guinness, and a splash of blackcurrant liquor. The drink was created in 1861 by a bartender in London to mourn the death of Prince Albert, who said even the champagne should be in mourning. The velvety texture of the champagne and Guinness proved to be delicious, and a popular cocktail to this very day! The drink is a bit of a novelty, and we love to serve in on New Year's Eve. This pairs particularly well with smoked salmon on scotch pancakes recipe!

COCKTAIL INGREDIENTS

4 ounces Guinness Irish stout
4 ounces champagne
1 tablespoon crème de cassis

HOW TO MAKE

1. Pour the champagne halfway into a tall, chilled champagne flute.

2. Slowly pour the Guinness beer on top of the champagne. This should float on top.

3. Top with the crème de cassis.

NOTE: One bottle of champagne and two bottles of Guinness will serve six guests.

Iced Irish Coffee

Serves 1

When the weather is warm and we need a caffein-ated fix, there is nothing better than an iced Irish coffee. The Irish cream dances an Irish jig in this iced coffee and steals the show! Add sugar to the coffee for preferred sweetness!

IRISH COFFEE INGREDIENTS

6 ounces coffee cold brewed coffee
2 ounces Irish cream liquor
1 ounce Irish whiskey
Ice

IRISH CREAM TOPPING INGREDIENTS

½ cup heavy cream
2 tablespoons Irish cream
1 tablespoon powdered sugar
Dark chocolate (shaved)

HOW TO MAKE

1. Brew fresh coffee and set it aside to cool in the refrigerator.

2. Whip the fresh cream, powdered sugar and Irish cream together for the topping and set aside. The cream topping will serve up to 4–6 people.

3. Fill a glass half full of ice.

4. Gently swirl together the Irish cream liquor and the Irish whiskey in a shaker with ice. Pour over the prepared chilled glass. Finally pour over the coffee and stir.

5. Top with Irish cream, chocolate shavings and serve with a straw.

Boozy Shamrock Shake

Who needs to wait until St. Patrick's Day to drink a Shamrock Shake? This minty boozy milkshake is a fun to drink especially in the summertime and the flavor is delicious!

SHAKE INGREDIENTS

1½ cups vanilla ice cream
3 tablespoons Irish cream
1½ tablespoons crème de menthe

GARNISH INGREDIENTS

Fresh whipped cream
Dash of vanilla
White chocolate (shaved)
Sprig of mint

HOW TO MAKE

1. Whip the cream with a dash of vanilla extract and set aside.
2. Add the vanilla ice cream, crème de menthe, Irish cream and vanilla extract into a blender and mix until smooth. Pour into a chilled glass and top with vanilla cream, white chocolate shavings and a sprig of fresh mint. Serve with a straw!

Final Words

Thank you for allowing me to guide you back to Ireland. I hope you have enjoyed this culinary journey as much as I have. My great grandparents never made it back to America after they returned to Ireland, so it felt as if my journey and, in many ways, this book, was a completion of a circle that began in 1896 on the windy shores of Donegal.

I love the legacy they left me and may I wish you every Joy in the Journey—until next time.

—Judith

Recipe Index